DATE

HOMELESS!

WITHOUT ADDRESSES IN AMERICA

By Cheryl Gorder

The Social Crisis of the Decade

50 CENTS DONATION WILL BE MADE FOR EACH BOOK SOLD!

Recipients to include:
Covenant House
National Coalition for the Homeless
Salvation Army

HOMELESS!

Without Addresses in America

Published by:

BLUE BIRD PUBLISHING
1713 East Broadway #306
Tempe AZ 85282
(602) 968-4088

© 1988 by Cheryl Gorder

ISBN 0-933025-11-4
$11.95

Cover art by Cheryl Gorder

Library of Congress Cataloging-in-Publication Data

Gorder, Cheryl, 1952-
　　　Homeless! :without addresses in America:
the social crisis of the decade.

　　　Bibliography: p.
　　　Includes index.
　　　1. Homelessness—United States. 2. Poor—
United States. I. Title.
HV4505.G67 1988　　　362.5'0973　　　88-22217
ISBN 0-933025-11-4

INTRODUCTION

Homelessness is a terrifying experience. It destroys families. It destroys self-confidence and even the will to live.

For the homeless, life becomes a desperate battle to survive. Every day becomes a struggle and the simplest things, such as giving your children a glass of milk or a candy bar, become an impossibility. And, fear is the constant companion of the homeless.

This fear especially impacts the children. Children need security. They need a home where they feel safe and where they are loved. But, homelessness deprives children of their natural joy and leaves them forever insecure.

If you have ever seen the look of fear in the face of the homeless, you will never forget it.

If you have seen a dirty little girl clinging to a tattered doll and watching the happy faces of the well-fed passing by, you will realize what homelessness is all about.

It is a terrible condition that is afflicting millions of Americans today. Families who were middle class and self-supporting have been reduced to poverty. Auto workers, miners, oil field workers and farmers have joined the ranks of the already poor.

It is a national tragedy.

Sumner Dodge
Director of Community Relations
Salvation Army
Southwest Regional Headquarters,
Phoenix, Arizona

TABLE OF CONTENTS

ACKNOWLEDGMENTS

The author would like to thank her family for support and patience during this project, and especially to her husband, Dale, and daughter, Sarah for ideas, photographs, and proofreading.

Many persons provided material and encouragement for this book. To the homeless persons who sat with me and told me about their lives—I thank you for letting the world know about your situations so that perhaps we can together find solutions. I would like to thank Geraldine Nieri of the Central Arizona Shelter System (CASS) for perserverance in helping me find photos for the book, and for putting me in touch with Jodi Abodeely, one of the photographers whose work appears in this book.

Thanks to Jodi Abodeely of Tarek Productions and Kira Corser not just for the photos, but also for having a sincere interest in helping the homeless.

A special thanks to Sumner Dodge of the Phoenix Salvation Army for providing photos, information about Salvation Army projects, and a touching introduction to this book.

Thanks to Covenant House for information and a photo of Father Bruce Ritter. And to Doubleday and Company, a division of Bantam, Doubleday, Dell Publishing Group, Inc. for permission to quote from *Covenant House* by Father Bruce Ritter, copyright 1987.

I appreciate the time that Chief Richard Voorhees of the Bridgewater, New Jersey police department took to give me information about project Home Free and also for providing a photograph of himself.

Also thanks to Macmillan Publishing Company for permission to quote from *The Other America* by Michael Harrington, copyright 1962.

𝕿𝖍𝖊 𝕬𝖙𝖑𝖆𝖓𝖙𝖆 𝕵𝖔𝖚𝖗𝖓𝖆𝖑-𝕮𝖔𝖓𝖘𝖙𝖎𝖙𝖚𝖙𝖎𝖔𝖓 kindly gave permission to reprint one of a series of articles by Lee Walburn entitled "Atlanta's streets a prison without walls for about 6,000," which appeared November 4, 1986.

I'm especially pleased that Ed Freska granted permission to reprint an editorial cartoon which I greatly admire.

Two other fine cartoonists granted permission to use their work: Drew Litton of the *Rocky Mountain News* and Mike Peters of the *Dayton Daily News*. We are proud to reprint their cartoons in this book.

I'd like to thank the *Christian Science Monitor* and photographer Neal Menschel for permission to use the photo of Jimmy and Rosalynn Carter working on the Habitat for Humanity project, and the photo of Habitat founder Millard Fuller.

Thanks to *The Arizona Republic* and staff photographer Suzanne Starr for permission to reprint one of her photos.

The US Conference of Mayors has been watching the issues of poverty, hunger and homelessness over the past few years, and produces regular reports. I'm grateful for access to the information they have faithfully gathered and made available to the public.

To the fine ladies of Mesa, Arizona, Doraine Frick and Lelia Parlier—I admire your charitable spirit. Your persistence will be rewarded.

And to all of the people who are giving of themselves in so many ways to help the homeless—your efforts are deeply appreciated.

AUTHOR'S INTRODUCTION

For the past fifteen years, my family and I have traveled the length and breadth of this country. During the last couple of years, we noticed a sharp change in the economy. We saw a change in the types of people we were seeing in the RV parks and campgrounds. It used to be mostly retired travelers or "snowbirds". Now it's becoming much more common to see young people, especially families, living in these campgrounds. They aren't tourists like the retired folks. The young families are living in whatever they can come up with- -tents, pop-up campers, pickup campers, buses, etc.

We also noticed more and more newspaper articles and TV reports about the large number of homeless people. Everywhere we went- -Charlotte, NC, Columbus, OH, Atlanta, Orlando, Fort Lauder- dale, Denver, Minneapolis, Dallas, Nashville, Boston, Phoenix, Seattle, there was something in the newspapers about homeless people. But yet if you talked to the public about the situation, no one knew anything about it. Most people seemed to be completely unaware of the homeless situation. *It's almost although these hundreds of thousands (perhaps millions) of homeless people are INVISIBLE!*

The plight of these many homeless people was obvious to me, but I realized that the rest of America needed to know the magnitude of the problem. People need to be informed about homelessness: why it's happening on such a large scale; who the homeless are; why 50% of today's homeless are families; why the old stereotype of "hobo" doesn't apply to most of the new American homeless population; how horrible it is to be on the streets; and what can be done about it. That's

CHAPTER ONE

NO HOME, NO HOPE

Say the word "homeless" to the average person on the street, and what is the reaction? "Worthless bums", or "hobos who don't give a hoot" are some of the comments you'll hear. The old stereotype of careless, perhaps carefree, panhandling, able-but-not-wanting-to-work hobos is still prevalent. Even though the new American homeless people do not fit into this description, that attitude prevails.

What is it about homelessness that people find so disagreeable? Is it their perceived weakness? Are we offended by their appearance visually, and by their situation emotionally to such an extent that we cannot cope with thinking about it? Do we fear that the same thing can happen to us? Are we afraid that their existence tears at the very fiber of the American success ethic?

To the average American, homelessness implies drinking too much, eating too little, sleeping too cold, and earning too little. A home implies stability, an anchor in a world of confusion and impermanence. Home is a refuge from the people and things that we find stressful or confusing.

A home means that we accept the mainstream values of American life. It says that we are acceptable. To be without a home makes people question your very right to exist. To be without a home is to be unacceptable. Or worse.

Today, to be without a home is to be invisible.

Americans don't realize the extent of homelessness in this nation **right now!** There are hundreds and hundreds of thousands (some say millions) of people who do not have a roof over their heads at night. There are children who have no place to call home. There are runaways with nowhere to go. There are mentally ill people with no facilities to care for them. They are real people with real problems, and there aren't enough places for them to go. One shelter volunteer said, "Most of the people I've met are normal people who've had normal jobs and led normal lives—until that moment they found themselves out on the street." And even if there was a place to go, there still wouldn't be any hope for their future.

This is America's tragedy! This is America's shame! A nation so rich and powerful that we set the standards for the rest of the world, yet there are people starving and homeless in our own land. How dare we set standards for the rest of the world when we are unable to meet those same standards at home.

A big problem lies in the fact that if we are to take care of the poor and the starving and the homeless, we must first admit that there are poor and hungry and homeless people. Americans tend to think everything is roses if they are allowed to get by with that type of thinking. People who have jobs and homes and cars and virtually everything they need don't want to stop to think about the less fortunate. It brings suffering too close to home if they have to admit that there are people who need help just a few blocks or a few miles away.

> **IT'S HARDER TO SEE POVERTY UNDER YOUR NOSE THAN TO SEE THE SUFFERING OF ANEMIC CHILDREN HALF A WORLD AWAY.**

It's also so much easier to help starving people on a different continent because we justify that "It's not their fault they're hungry. They had a drought." Or "Their government doesn't care about poor people". If we have to admit that there's poverty right under our noses, then we have to stop and think about what's wrong right here at home. There's no severe droughts causing hunger. So obviously the fault lies within us or our system. Isn't it awful to have to place the blame on oneself!

This book will make you do both. It will tell you that there is homelessness in large amounts here in the United States. It will also tell you that we the people are to blame. We are to blame for the government policies we allow to be passed and we are to blame for not seeing it sooner.

HOW MANY HOMELESS?

Estimates of the total homeless population in the United States vary from a low of 250,000 to 350,000, the administration's estimates, to 3,000,000, the figure advanced by the Committee for Creative Non-Violence. Mitch Snyder of this Committee, based in Washington DC, believes that 1% of the population of the United States is homeless. He testified before a congressional committee studying homelessness. The congressional committee eventually concluded, after hearing further testimony, that the US Department of Housing and Urban Development (HUD) figures were "gross underestimates". Nevertheless, it's difficult to accurately count the number of homeless, because they don't show up on anyone's reports. They are "invisible".

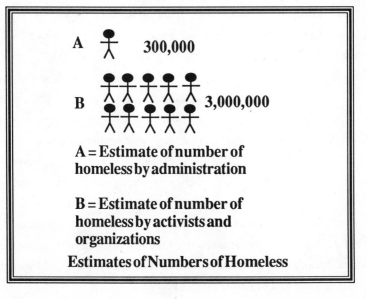

A � 300,000

B ����� 3,000,000

A = Estimate of number of
homeless by administration

B = Estimate of number of
homeless by activists and
organizations

Estimates of Numbers of Homeless

One thing is for sure, though. The homeless population is growing by leaps and bounds. Most cities say the numbers of homeless within their city limits have doubled in the last two, three, or five years. Charleston, South Carolina, has double the homeless in 1987 than they had in 1986. Dover, Delaware, has stated that the demand for their shelter services has doubled in two years.Studies predict that homelessness will double again within three years.

The US Conference of Mayors in 1987 showed that requests for emergency shelter have been on the increase in 29 of the 31 cities studied. San Francisco showed a 100% increase in the past year, and Providence, Rhode Island, reported a 70% increase.

Major cities show mammoth populations of homeless. New York City is estimated to have 30,000; Los Angeles: 33,000; Chicago: 25,000. (See Chart.) Smaller cities also have proportionately large numbers of homeless: Newark, New Jersey: 8,000; Cleveland, Ohio: 6,000; Phoenix, Arizona: 4,000; Huntington, West Virginia: 175; Reno, Nevada: 1,200.

But large cities are not the only ones with people living without roofs. Homelessness is a problem in such places as Fargo, North Dakota; Des Moines, Iowa; Asheville, North Carolina; Clarksville Tennessee; Lewiston, Maine; Topeka, Kansas; Helena, Montana; Burlington, Vermont; and Lorain, Ohio. (See Map.)

Homelessness is not confined to just a few cities or a few states. It is not just a momentary problem, and it does not occur just in the winter in the sunbelt states. Right now, homelessness is in epidemic proportions. One source has called the problem "the initial tidal wave". Many others have said that it's just the tip of the iceberg—that we will be seeing more and more homelessness in the next few years. Not since the Depression have so many people been without homes.

In 1949, the government promised every citizen a decent dwelling. For a while, it seemed as though low-housing projects were putting roofs over the heads of the poor. Great improvements were made in the way low-income people lived. Hunger seemed to diminish and poor children seemed healthier. But the trend has been reversed, due a gradual encroachment on low-income housing and gradual cutbacks in federal spending for social programs. These changes took place slowly until one day— POOF!—there's lots and lots of homeless people.

SAMPLING OF HOMELESS POPULATIONS IN SELECTED CITIES

Los Angeles	33,000	New York City	30,000
Chicago	25,000	Dallas	13,000
Philadelphia	10,000	Denver	10,000
Cincinnati	9,000	Miami	8,000
Newark, NJ	8,000	Cleveland	6,000
Atlanta	6,000	Boston	5,000
Santa Clara, CA	5,000	Phoenix	4,000
Alameda County, CA	4,000	New Orleans	4,000
Long Beach, CA	4,000	San Francisco	3,000
Seattle	3,000	Tucson	3,000
Memphis	2,000	Albuquerque	2,000
Westchester, CT	1,600	Fresno County, CA	1,300
Des Moines	1,200	Reno	1,200
Salt Lake City	1,000	Portland	1,000
Knoxville	1,000	Patterson, NJ	880
Nashville	670	Topeka	300
Huntington, WV	175	Asheville, NC	125

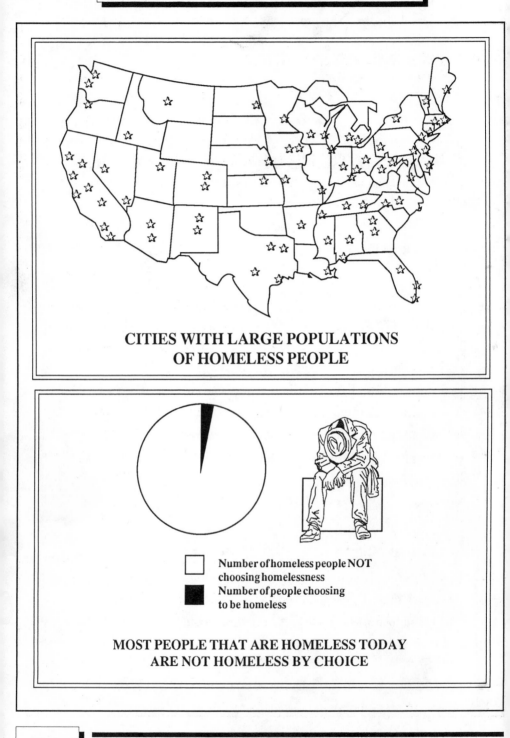

**CITIES WITH LARGE POPULATIONS
OF HOMELESS PEOPLE**

Number of homeless people NOT
choosing homelessness

Number of people choosing
to be homeless

**MOST PEOPLE THAT ARE HOMELESS TODAY
ARE NOT HOMELESS BY CHOICE**

THE NEW HOMELESS: FAMILIES

The profile of the typical American homeless is not the same as the 1950's. Then it was the chronic transients, "hobos", who made up the bulk of homeless people. They were often homeless by choice. Many had chronic problems, such as alcoholism. Others simply chose a gypsy lifestyle and "rode the rail". Hobo camps by the railroad tracks were not uncommon. These "camps" generally were a temporary home to just a few men. Not many women chose this lifestyle.

Today, many homeless people are women, children, and teenagers. Whole families are now being forced out into the street for lack of affordable housing. Half of the people without homes today are families.

"Now we're seeing working people—young married couples who cannot afford available housing," said Kevin Hooper of the Salvation Army shelter in Delaware. He stresses the lack of housing as the root cause for the increase in homeless families. Half of today's homeless are families, which could mean as many as one and a half **million** people.

A survey of 29 cities by the United States Conference of Mayors said that the "most significant difference" in the homeless population is the growing number of families with children. They are one- or two-parent families with children. Some are unemployed, others underemployed. Most have been evicted from their homes. Some are former factory workers whose jobs have been terminated due to economic changes. Some are displaced middle-aged homemakers with teenage children who have been abandoned by male breadwinners. Others are young women with children whose boyfriends have deserted them.

"Not only does the old stereotype of the broken-down male wino no longer apply, but increasingly, the stereotypical homeless person in America is a small child," said Maria Foscarinis, legal counsel for the National Coalition for the Homeless.

Many times the breadwinner of these families has a job, but an emergency causes them to miss rent payments. If a member of the family gets sick, it's often enough of a burden to cause them to eventually become evicted. "A third to half the people we see coming in for emergency shelter are working," noted Tina Narr of the Seattle-King County Emergency Housing Coalition.

Many tent cities have sprung up all over the nation.

impa...

A minimum wage job just won't cover basic necessities, and the poor often have to choose between food and shelter. Cutbacks in federal programs hurt these people the most. Even a small change in income can mean the difference between a home and the streets.

Homelessness is not limited to poor people who have problems. People with incomes over the poverty level also can end up in the streets. "Most people in America are only two paychecks away from the streets," noted Betti Knott, director of the St. Vincent de Paul Society.

The homeless are becoming younger and younger. More than half are under the age of 35, many of these are between 20 and 30 years of age. The average age is 29. Thirteen percent are under the age of 19. That leaves roughly one third over the age of 35. Thirty years ago, most homeless people were over the age of 60.

The homeless are better educated people than ever before. Half are high school graduates. One in five has attended college. One in twenty has a college degree.

Obviously, these are not the stereotypical male hobo. And obviously typical bandage solutions are not enough to solve this problem. "It's almost like it was in the Depression," stated Betti Knott. "It's frightening."

"None of them ever thought they were going to end up here," said one shelter worker. Through misfortune or federal policy, and usually a combination of the two, thousands and thousands of families are without permanent shelter.

important

> "None of them ever thought they were going to end up here."

THE NEW HOMELESS: MENTALLY ILL

Another large portion of today's American homeless is the mentally ill people who have no place to go. Several years ago, the United States began a policy of "deinstitutionalization"; which succinctly means that less people were going to be committed to mental institutions and that their visits would be shorter. These institutions were encouraged to let their patients back into mainstream life as soon as possible. For many, there was nowhere to go once back in society at large.

About one third of the homeless population is the mentally ill. If there are three million homeless persons in the United States, then there are one million mentally ill people without permanent shelter. A Ohio study showed that one third of the homeless polled had been in a psychiatric hospital before living on the streets. Half of these mentally ill people had been discharged within the past two years.

In 1955 there were 560,000 patients in state mental hospitals. By 1985, that number had dropped to 116,000. That's not because less people need treatment now than in 1985. It's because the policy dictates that fewer people are committed to these hospitals, and for a shorter time. This policy has been in effect since the 1960's.

The trend toward earlier discharge of psychiatric hospital patients has come partly from a sense that a hospital stay does more harm than good and partly from the lack of funds to care for indigent patients. Economic factors had a great influence in the decision to treat fewer patients and for shorter periods of time.

Local mental health centers were supposed to be the main sources of treatment for released patients who were trying to get back into the mainstream of society. Because of lack of funds, these centers are often unable to treat the very people they were created for. Many of the people in need of mental health treatment end up in shelters instead of the clinics. Thus they are not provided adequate follow-up treatment or supervision. Some are too sick or disorganized to understand their situation.

People who are clearly mentally ill cannot be forcibly hospitalized unless they commit an act of danger to themselves or to others. They can be chronically ill, but not receive any treatment at all. So "deinstitutionalization", which sought to move people who are not a danger to themselves or others back into the community, had the effect of dumping thousands of incapacitated people into the streets. This inhumane policy has been called "dumping" for obvious reasons. These people may not have needed permanent confinement such as provided by state mental hospitals, but they obviously need special help in organizing their lives.

The community mental health services are unprepared to deal with and treat the psychotic homeless people. There are an insufficient number of halfway houses, and many patients do not have families to turn to. Funding that had been planned for community mental health services often failed to materialize, even after patients had been released from the state institutions.

THE NEW HOMELESS: RUNAWAYS

A large number of homeless teenage runaways now haunts the streets. An ABC News Nightline report found that since 1977, there have always been at least 500,000 homeless runaways, and at times possibly as many as 2,000,000. In New York City, there are 15,000; in Atlanta, 3,000; in Dallas, 4,000; in Washington DC, 5,000; and in Los Angeles, 12,000.

These are America's invisible children. They belong to no one now. This vast, but secret population is a story that doesn't go away. And this story has especially gruesome endings. Unlike homeless families, who might find help or a way out of their situation, homeless runaways often end up dead. They face special problems because of their youth and vulnerability. They are easy pickings for the worst criminal element in our cities.

These discarded youth face disintegration in their values. Most will not find a way out. They can't survive the streets. They need a way to be able to complete their growing up before being thrust into the realities of such hardships. They need to be reached quickly so that they can be saved.

THESE ARE AMERICA'S INVISIBLE CHILDREN. THEY BELONG TO NO ONE NOW. THIS VAST, BUT SECRET POPULATION IS A STORY THAT DOESN'T GO AWAY.

THE HOMELESS PROFILE

oday's American homeless population is comprised primarily of families, mentally ill persons, and runaways. These millions of people are generally invisible to society, or at least ignored. News media does pay attention to their plight, but often not until cold weather strikes. And usually the only time the rest of America notices them is in time to provide a hearty Thanksgiving meal for every poor person in the country. There's something about the American conscience that wants to see everyone fed at least two days a year: Thanksgiving and Christmas. And a toy for every child. But other than that, our collective conscience does not seem to generate enough interest to *solve* the problems causing homelessness. We simply feed it on holidays.

The old stereotypes do not apply any more to today's homeless. It's not just a wino on the corner who doesn't care anyway. More often than not, it's a man with a wife and two children, or a single mother with more than she can handle, or a mentally disturbed woman, or a runaway teenager.

"This is becoming a societal problem and people cannot keep ignoring the people on the street," said Michael Moreau, director of the Travelers Aid Society of New Orleans. "People who never dreamed of being evicted, of losing their job, of being without food and shelter are finding themselves in the ranks of the economically exiled."

Through misfortune or economic forces, these people have fallen from the American mainstream. "Some of them are very sophisticated and well-dressed. When they come up to the table you say to yourself, 'Whoa!' You can't go by what they look like," was the comment by a volunteer in one of San Jose's food kitchens.

"Homelessness is a wider phenomenon than the public may have been aware," said Bernie Jones, professor of planning and community development at the University of Colorado in Denver. Understated, but true. Homelessness is in epidemic proportions; yet the general public seems totally unaware of any problem.

One minister commented that "even a convicted murderer is given a bed to sleep on, food to eat, and a roof over his head."

Compassion is needed; action is needed. We need to change our stereotypical attitudes about homelessness, and then we need to do something about the policies

Contrary to popular belief, most of the people who are homeless actually DO NOT choose to be homeless!

REASONS FOR HOMELESSNESS

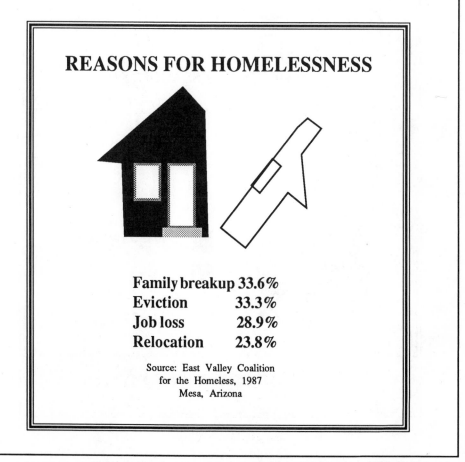

Family breakup 33.6%
Eviction 33.3%
Job loss 28.9%
Relocation 23.8%

Source: East Valley Coalition
for the Homeless, 1987
Mesa, Arizona

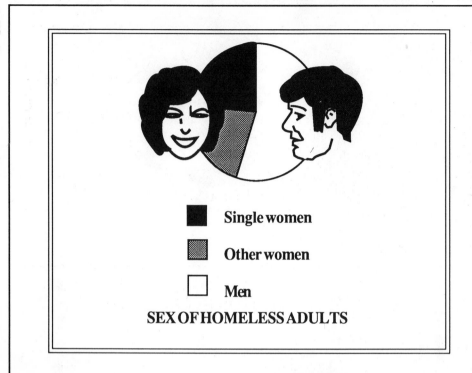

SEX OF HOMELESS ADULTS

- Single women
- Other women
- Men

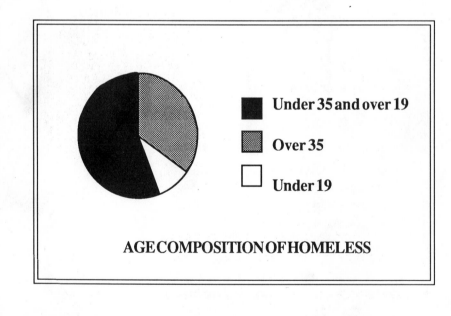

- Under 35 and over 19
- Over 35
- Under 19

AGE COMPOSITION OF HOMELESS

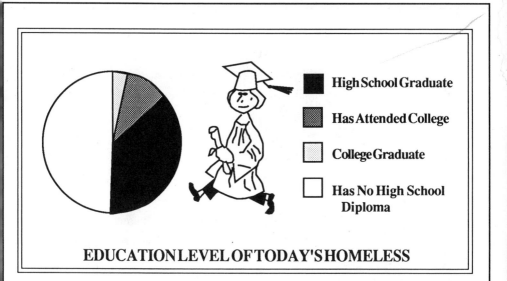

EDUCATION LEVEL OF TODAY'S HOMELESS

- High School Graduate
- Has Attended College
- College Graduate
- Has No High School Diploma

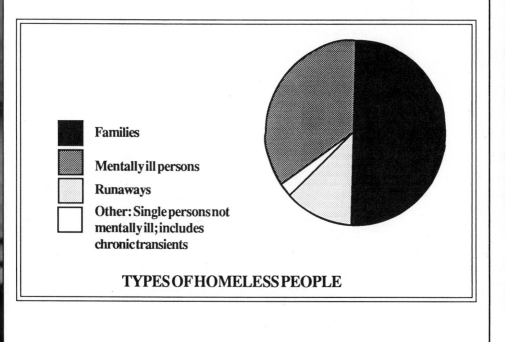

- Families
- Mentally ill persons
- Runaways
- Other: Single persons not mentally ill; includes chronic transients

TYPES OF HOMELESS PEOPLE

which cause it. Long-term solutions are not shelters, although they are needed now. Long-term solutions are low income housing, help for the mentally disturbed, and help for runaways. And of course, a long-term commitment to caring enough not to let it happen again.

A GENERATION FROM NOW

A generation ago, a book drew attention to the forgotten side of America. *The Other America: Poverty in the United States* showed affluent Americans that there really was poverty and hunger in America, and in enormous quantities. Author Michael Harrington then pleaded:

> *After one reads the facts, either there are anger and shame, or there are not. And, as usual, the fate of the poor hangs upon the decision of the better-off. If this anger and shame are not forthcoming, some- one can write a book about the other America a generation from now and it will the the same, or worse.*

Let us not have to repeat this warning, a generation from now.

CHAPTER TWO:

WHAT IS IT LIKE TO BE HOMELESS?

O nly the homeless know what it's like to be living on the streets. The rest of us can only use our imagination to try to sense the feelings that the homeless know so well. That's why Lee Walburn, a staff writer for **The Atlanta Journal**, left the comfort of his home to live on the streets. He wanted to be totally aware of how homelessness affects all of a person's senses: how it looks, how it smells, what it feels like inside. He did not want to write about homelessness from the outside, but from the inside. The articles he produced from this experience are truly amazing. They project the sense of frustration and pain that is not evident to the passer-by.

The following is one day's feature from this series. It appeared on November 4, 1986. We are grateful to **The Atlanta Journal** for permission to reprint it.

Atlanta's streets a prison without walls for about 6,000
By Lee Walburn

After almost a week of living with Atlanta's homeless I began to view the streets as a prison without tangible confinement.

Like any prisoner, I did not want to remain in my degradation another minute. But, had I not been automatically lifted from the situation by the ending of a newspaper assignment, I would have only been able to ask in bewilderment, "Which way is out?"

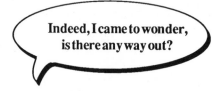

Indeed, I came to wonder, is there any way out?

Indeed, I came to wonder, is there any way out?

The three elements necessary to function in American society are money, food, and shelter. Of the three, food is the most readily available on the streets once you learn the routine. The other two require regular resourcefulness.

Food I had found the first night through the grace of The Open Door on Ponce de Leon [Street]. Such beneficence at suppertime would not be available on a regular basis because the shelter is designed for 18 permanent residents. Supper, I would find, is an everyday problem.

Shelter, from the start, was even more of an enigma. On my first day, it was too late to get into the Salvation Army mission on Luckie Street for the one free night offered there. The Union Mission off the south end of Pryor, which will establish a charge account, was too far away to walk to.

At The Open Door I met a man named Robert, who said he would spend the first night on the street with me. I was grateful for his companionship because I was frightened. With Robert's friend, Jordan, we walked through an alley and headed toward the railroad tracks that crossed Ponce de Leon near the old baseball field where the Atlanta Crackers once played.

In the alley was a cinder-block building with a giant heart and cupid's arrow painted on the side. Moonshine is sometimes available here for the homeless who have accumulated a few coins. With too little money to rent a room, they buy momentary forgetfulness in a jar.

Near Piedmont Park, Jordan found a quarter. Less than 10 minutes later he found a paperback book, "The Cat Who Ate Modern Danish." He dropped each into a pocket of his old coat.

Too frightened to claim urban 'cave'

In the inner city we discovered a variety of "cat holes" and "caves," names given to abandoned buildings and crevices between skyscrapers or holes in walls of kudzu. Most smelled of urine. Those that were not occupied we were too frightened to claim.

We walked for several hours to ward off the growing chill. We stopped in the Dunk 'n Dine on Peachtree [Street]. The worker there gave us three glasses of water without comment on our failure to order food. Jordan used his quarter to help finance a cup of coffee for himself. We used the restroom. We chatted with a woman named Carol. She asked if anybody had seen old Dave from Wisconsin.

Back on the streets we fell in behind two men who looked to be in their 50s. They were fresh shaven and their clothes did not stink. They smelled of cheap wine. The black-haired man moved to the middle of the street and pretended to be roller-skating. The both laughed.

The night grew colder—coldest since last spring. Back on the streets, we checked several well-known air vents downtown, but none was blowing warm air. Robert suggested that we look for a place to rest near Grady Memorial Hospital.

In front of the Fulton County health building, someone had left a large sheet of cardboard. "A bed," exulted Robert.

We slept fitfully, although seemingly not at all. We slept with bodies touching in the manner of the street, so that if one awoke, all did. Several times we sensed strange presences and sat up startled.

One of the strangers, J.C. Bush, said he planned to stand there awhile before resuming his walking. He spat tobacco juice into the bushes. He said he had been on the streets "since I got kicked outa the church place 'cause I got drunk." He said it had been two days since he had been drunk.

He spat again into the shrubbery and then started to walk away. "Maybe they open up the winder shelters early this year since it's so cold," he said.

Fully awake now, we strolled into the lobby of Grady and used the restroom. A guard saw us and came to lock the restroom door once we were out. "You can't stay here," she said.

At 4 a.m., no longer able to stand the cold, we decided to try Grady's emergency room. Thirty minutes later, the warmness having put me to sleep, I was awakened by a guard who said, "You got a blue [admission] slip? Then you can't stay here."

"You can't stay here."

Only young and strong called for jobs

The three of us walked, waiting for the labor pool on Spring Street to open. When we got there, several men were snoring on chairs pulled together under signs that said, "No Sleeping Here."

"Only signs," a man said as he assembled three hard-back chairs for his own use.

Rap music blared from a radio. The smell of old socks was pervasive. A craps game broke out in a corner. Soon two of the men were arguing over a dollar.

Periodically names were called and the persons responding were assigned jobs and given instructions on how to get there. Others pleaded with the boss on a platform, "C'mon, I need it, man."

My name was not called. It was evident that only the names of the young and the strong would be called. A large man walked around and said, "I need workers with boots. If you ain't working, hit the bricks."

I could not have worked had I been called. I was hungry and without sleep. I would have had to go to work without any food and I would have returned too late to obtain a free meal at any of the soup kitchens.

It would not take many days of such a routine to convince any rational person that it was more advantageous to stay near the soup kitchens than to seek a job at one of the many labor pools.

Wages from the jobs dispensed there are consistently

minimal. There is often a charge for transportation to and from the job. Sometimes equipment has to be rented. Lunch must be paid for from the earnings.

There are fewer than 150 free suppers available each night. Supper, if there is any, takes a priority of $5 if any degree of nutrition is a priority.

Then comes the choice of renting a room from what remains of the wages and perhaps investing in basic hygiene materials, or saving it for food the next day when you may not be chosen for a job. Laborers are rarely chosen three consecutive days.

The labor pools can be dehumanizing. One morning in a building near the Butler Street CME Church, where many of the street people go for breakfast, a young man was squatting behind a row of chairs. He was drinking a Colt malt liquor partially covered by a brown sack and was soliciting the favor of a woman dressed in rags. She tried to ignore him. There was heavy activity around the platform. There was shuffling and frequently the anthem from another age, "Yeah, boss."

Rookie has little chance scavenging

One man complained because he hadn't gotten an assignment. "Didn't I take care of you yesterday, nigger?" he was asked.

Since few old-timers are chosen for the work force, the most reliable ways to raise money are collecting aluminum cans for recycling and selling plasma.

I tried my hand at scavenging for aluminum. A rookie has little chance. After a couple of hours I estimated I had less than 2 pounds. Even if I had had enough energy to walk to a reclamation center, what can you buy with less than 50 cents? I realized that I needed a system and gave up.

The plasma banks are the best bet for oldsters. After a nap in a sunlit corner of the city library and lunch at St. Luke's soup kitchen on Peachtree [Street], I approached Medical Plasma on Simpson Street. Immediately I was set upon by a black man hustling with the practiced patter of a used-car salesman.

"First time? Eight bucks and five as a bonus. After that,

$11. Twice a week. All you need is an ID."

I told him I didn't have an ID and moved on. Had I not been acting, it would have been only a matter of days before I was back. Plasma is the only steady money if you are too young for government benefits and too old to be chosen at the labor pool or your feet hurt too badly to walk in search of cans.

Although prospects for me were slim at the employment office, at least it was warm and a refuge until breakfast. I returned twice, applied and rested. I was never chosen.

A line for food at any time of the day holds the dynamics for violence. But breakfast is a blueprint for hell. Faces buried too often in the crook of an elbow laid hard against the concrete are lined like road maps. Eyes are red as coals. Breath is like a backed-up sewer. Hands shake more in the morning, perhaps in the dread of what is to follow.

> **A LINE FOR FOOD AT ANY TIME OF THE DAY HOLDS THE DYNAMICS FOR VIOLENCE. BUT BREAKFAST IS A BLUEPRINT FOR HELL.**

One at a time or in pairs, never in groups, they slouch away toward the next warmness and the next supply of fuel for their bodies.

Some may be lucky enough to find irregular employment and work their way into paid shelters such as the Salvation Army or the Union Mission. One in 500 may make it all the way to his own apartment and gainful employment.

The distance from wandering without any purpose on the streets to even the Salvation Army and its bunkhouse cots, baths, and two meals is a gigantic leap. The difference in sleeping in a room with 20 snoring men and sleeping on the streets or splintered floor is the difference between numbing fatigue and mere tiredness. With tiredness, there is hope. With fatigue, nothing.

> **WITH TIREDNESS, THERE IS HOPE.**
> **WITH FATIGUE, NOTHING.**

CHAPTER THREE:

FACES OF HOMELESSNESS

Home Street Home is an exhibit of photographs with accompanying poetry. This exhibit forms a personal understanding of homeless persons as individuals. The exhibit has appeared in the Rotunda of the Senate in Washington D.C., in the John F. Kennedy School of Government at Harvard University, in the California State Capitol Building, and at the Memorial Union Gallery at Arizona State University. There is a companion book to the exhibit.

The photographer of *Home Street Home,* Kira Corser, has kindly granted permission to reprint her photos in this chapter.

Food Line, Cedar Community Center,
First Presbyterian Church.

Handle with care

Measuring Homelessness

Numbers cannot count
the pain of hunger,
the dread of tomorrow.
Numbers cannot see
the sleepless nights,
the aching bones.
Charts don't show
a child's tearful embrace,
the parents' weariness.
Statistics cannot feel
the longing, the loneliness.

If they could, the numbers
would shoot off the pages
The charts would reach the
skies and people's hearts
could finally
measure homelessness.

Bag man. "I live like a person."

Lydia, U.S.A.

Francisco, "I was the Golden Boy."

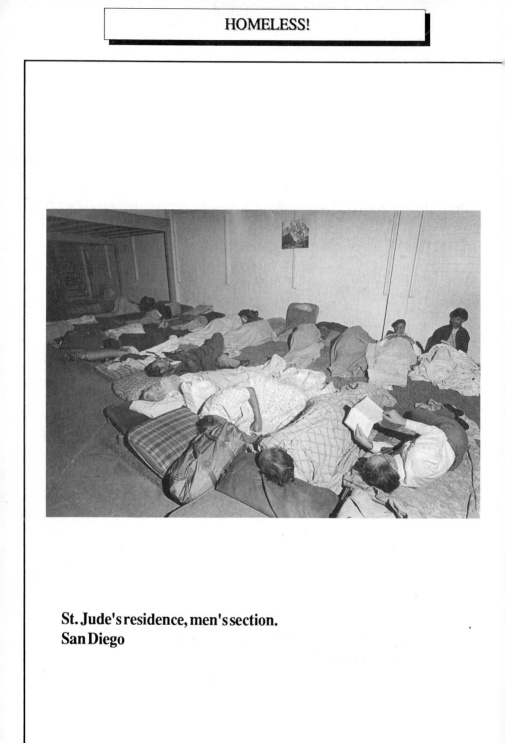

St. Jude's residence, men's section.
San Diego

St. Jude's residence, women's section.
An old tire factory, 300 people sleep on the floor.
Closed for lack of funds, May 1984.

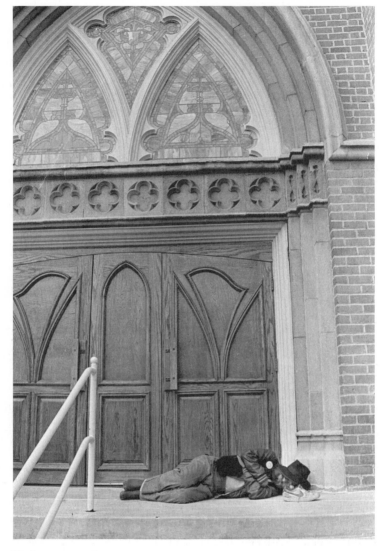

No home, no hope.

America's castoffs.

Jesse, sleeping at the public library.

Charles, "Move on."

Anita, "I don't understand."

Jake, "I'm mighty damn slow."

Dorothy, "I believe people too much."

Marilyn, a mirror of herself.

The good life.

The Good Life

They say
GNP is up, up, up.
They say
more people have jobs.
They say
it's a fine economic recovery.
They say....
They say....
But we feel....
We feel....

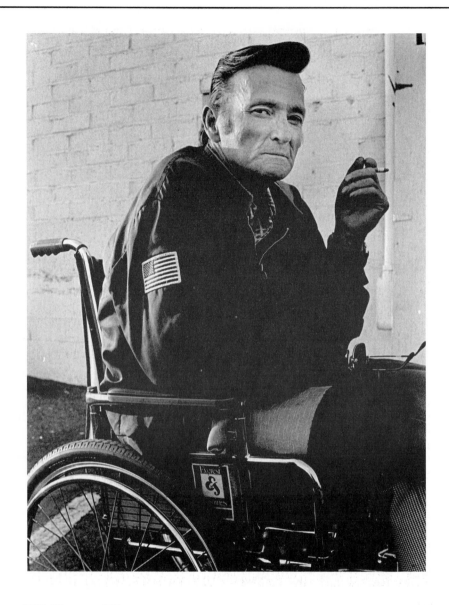

Bill, Korean War vet, three purple hearts.

Hillcrest

View from window.

View from window.

"ONE WAY."
Easter food line

Easter Food Line

Bright and early Easter morning
Let's put on our Easter bonnets
And stroll the Easter parade.

Mommy, why are all those people
standing in line over there?

Honey, it's just people needing food
today....

What about tomorrow, Mommy?
When our Easter bonnets are put away?

WHAT DO THE HOMELESS LOOK LIKE?

THEY LOOK LIKE YOU AND ME.

The Invisible Americans

Why is there no way
to really see
these people.
Our eyes are open,
or are they?

CHAPTER FOUR

THE NEW HOMELESS: FAMILIES

Tom B.'s wife was pregnant last year when she quit her job to take care of their three other children. Soon after, he lost his warehouse job. A series of misfortunes landed them in a local church-supported shelter.

When he first lost his job, Tom was able to draw some unemployment while he continued to look for work. When that ran out, both he and his wife were actively looking for any sort of job that would pay real money. They found none, and the money ran out completely. They could no longer pay the rent.

They packed their belongings and stored them with a friend. The first night was spent in their car, and the children were washed for school at a fast food chain. They moved into a motel that was $33 a night, which meant every day they had to come up with real cash to pay the motel. Each job had to be a cash and carry ordeal, which usually meant a different job every day.

Tom woke each day wondering how the family was going to make it through the day. His wife made it through each day by keeping everyone else organized, but the stress grew as each morning the children asked, "Will we be home tonight, Mommy?"

Matters grew worse when their "friend" sold their belongings and skipped town. Then their car conked out and they didn't have any money to fix it. That was the day before their fourth child was born.

They could not keep paying the money for the motel because of all of the expenses of the new baby. They had nowhere else to turn except to the local shelter. Although Tom has had work almost regularly, it's still not enough to make the deposits they need to move into an apartment plus buy food and keep the car running.

"We never thought this would happen to us," said Mrs. B.

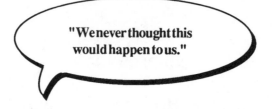

"We never thought this would happen to us."

Nobody ever does think that it could happen to them. A steady job is like a buffer between a person and reality—what life could be like without the security of a steady paycheck. But as hundreds of thousands of people have discovered in recent years, that steady paycheck is no longer dependable.

In the San Francisco Bay Area, thousands of people were put out of work when first General Motors, then Ford, each closed plants. In the once-booming Silicon Valley, more than 11,000 people were laid off in 1985. Many people who had never before been near the poverty level saw it for the first time. Tied into the area through mortgages and other connections, they struggled to meet every obligation without income.

Ted and his wife Felicia and their two sons were one such family. After being laid off from jobs they thought would last forever, they were able to meet their bills for several months. They tightened their spending habits and made only purchases of absolute necessity. Eventually though, they found that it was a strain just to pay the monthly utilities. Their payment on their two-bedroom home was $700 a month, and that alone was a problem now.

All around them, friends and relatives were packing up and leaving. Many of them just abandoned their mortgages, knowing full well they could not pay it without a job. Others were filing for bankruptcy. Ted and Felicia hung on with tooth and nail.

Finally the strain was too much. Their savings was gone. There was no more money and no more hope for any income. Their meager earnings from what work they could find was nowhere near enough to pay for their home. They had sold everything they had of any value. Ted even sold the rifle given to him by his dad just before he died. Their home now was completely bare except for a few skeleton pieces of furniture: beds, a couch, and a kitchen table.

Their decision to leave the Bay Area was one of necessity. They heard rumors of work in Oregon, so they headed up the coast. They found rent to be cheap there, but the rumors of work turned out to be empty promises.

Scraping together enough gas money, they headed for Arizona where there was supposed to be plenty of jobs. When they arrived in Phoenix, the first news to greet them was that there were already 6,000 homeless people in the Valley of the Sun. Already 6,000 people without homes, most without jobs! They wept.

Standing in the food line, Felicia said that the hardest part was on the children, "They don't know who they are now. My boys, they are confused. I'm scared, but I can't let it show."

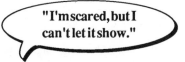

Most of the homeless families never thought that it could happen to them. Most of them came from stable lives with jobs, paychecks, security. They were used to working hard and earning a fair living, even if at times they were in a financial pinch. But they never expected to end up on the streets.

The growing number of homeless families has been of major concern to the United States Conference of Mayors. Today, many homeless people are women and children. Some are one- or two- parent families. Some are employed, others underemployed. Some are people whose jobs have been terminated due to economic changes. Others are divorced middle-aged mothers with few job skills. Some are young mothers abandoned by the father of their children. Some are doubling up with families and friends until "they can make it on their own."

Half of the homeless people today are families, not the old stereotypical "hobo" riding the rail. That means as many as one and a half million homeless people are families. And none of them thought they could end up like this. Shelter authorities have likened it to the Depression. The National Coalition for the Homeless, in their report "Saving Lives: Emergency Federal Aid Reaches the Streets", November, 1987, said that, "Families with children represent the fastest growing segment of this [homeless] population—accounting for a third to a half of all homeless persons."

WHO ARE THESE HOMELESS FAMILIES?

Data on homeless families has been given by the Homeless Families and Children Project in Atlanta. They found that of the homeless families aided in that city:

☆ 83% were headed by single females

☆ 43% were employed but not able to make it on their salaries

☆ 60% of the children were under the age of 5

☆ the average number of children was 2

☆ parents' average age was 29

☆ only 36% had been on welfare programs previously

Volunteers accumulating this data believed that a larger percentage of the households would have been headed by two parents if financial stress had not contributed to a breakup.

"The numbers are staggering," said Sharon Wiggins of the Junior League of Atlanta. She believes that most people are not aware of the awesome number of women with children who are homeless.

Most of these people are experiencing homelessness for the first time. "These are not typical street people," said one shelter director. And her associate added, "We're seeing more and more women with young children. They all have basically the same story: their husband left them and the kids."

Atlanta is not unique in this problem of homeless families. Cities all over the United States report similar findings. In Cincinnati, of 1806 homeless persons surveyed, 320 were children and 358 were women. In Louisville, the fastest growing poverty group is female-headed households and 75% of the calls to the American Family Emergency Shelter are from single mothers, most of them in their mid-20s. In Dallas, a brand new program to help the homeless found that it served 250 families in one month. In that same city, the number of families seeking help from food cooperatives and emergency services jumped 75% in one year. Burlington, Vermont, officials found that 60% of the homeless families they see are led by single mothers.

In southern California, Arizona, and Florida, public and private campgrounds are full of families in tents, pop-up campers, buses, pickup campers, or anything similar. These are not weekend vacationers. This is their life. They have found they cannot afford traditional housing and are trying to put a roof over their heads even if it's nonconventional.

In many places, camping families are discouraged or frowned upon. Sometimes there is a limit the the number of days a family can stay. In the Orange County, California, parks, campers may stay 15 days a month or 180 days a year. In California state parks, no one may camp for more than 30 days total in a year. Some campgrounds restrict visitors by age limitations, such as "snowbird" campgrounds that allow only senior citizens or at least no one under the age of 18. There are also common restrictions against tenters, pop-up campers, and converted buses that are aimed against live-ins.

Photo: Courtesy of Salvation Army

Today, many homeless people are women and children.

THE US CONFERENCE OF MAYORS

The problem of homeless families is so crucial that it has been a major focus of the United States Conference of Mayors for the past three years.Their December 1986 report "The Continued Growth of Hunger, Homelessness and Poverty in America's Cities: 1986" states that "families with children comprise 76% of the homeless population in New York City." And in Portland, 52% of the people served by an emergency housing program were families with children. Half of the homeless people in Philadelphia, Trenton and Yonkers are families. Forty percent of the homeless population in Chicago and Kansas City are families. Significant percentages of the homeless population in other major cities are also families.

Of the 25 cities surveyed in 1986, many noticed a significant change in the types of people that are homeless in recent years. "The most significant difference has been a growing number of families with children, with 80% of the cities reporting an increase among this group."

City officials responding to the survey noted:

Chicago: "There are more homeless families with children. More families are breaking down due to unemployment, stress, and abuse, and are requesting shelter from the city."

Phoenix: "We are seeing more homeless families than ever before."

Philadelphia: "The single most significant change has been the unwavering increase each year in the number of families who are homeless. We are approaching a point at which almost 50% of the persons in shelters are families with children—a horrifying statistic."

THE WORKING HOMELESS

A shocking observation about today's homeless is how many are employed, but not earning enough to put a roof over their family's heads. "They squeaked by financially in the past, but now, because of some emergency, they can't squeak by anymore," said Reverend Bridgford of the Urban Outreach Ministry of Norfolk, Virginia.

This class of "working poor" is between a rock and a hard spot. Often they do not qualify for any aid, even though they are homeless. If their income is above $8,277 annual income, they cannot receive federal aid. Yet that amount may not be enough to cover soaring housing costs. For instance, average rent for a two-bedroom apartment in the San Francisco Bay area is $700 or more. Add to that all of the security deposits, cleaning deposits, utility deposits, and an income of $1060 by a homeless person will not cover moving into an apartment for several months. In the meantime, any emergency could wipe out savings made.

A typical working family with children, not receiving any aid, can easily see their monthly paychecks eaten up in two days by a car payment, insurance, diapers, and food. Between soaring costs, and tightening of eligibility for federal food programs, these working people get left out in the cold—**literally.**

When the economy went down, so did aid programs. So the people who needed help most during the bad times were not able to get it. And large number of families dropped below the poverty level, making the need even greater. More and more people are "falling through the cracks" of our system. Thus a whole new concept of "poor" has been created—the homeless working poor. Even if they eventually can afford housing, there is a good chance that they will periodically and regularly become homeless.

The working poor are perilously close to becoming permanently homeless. All it takes is an accident, an illness, or any crisis that would be minor to someone with more substantial means to deal with it. Even the car breaking down can be enough to force the working poor into the streets.

James Rouse, chairman of the National Housing Task Force, reported to Congress in April, 1988, "Behind the homeless on the street are millions of Americans

ONE IN EVERY THREE HOMELESS PERSONS HAS A JOB—"THE WORKING POOR"

who are right on the edge, and could be on the street tomorrow if they lost their jobs or had a medical emergency." This housing report is the third in recent months to express that today's homelessness is only the "tip of a very dangerous iceberg," according to *Time Magazine,* April 11, 1988.

In Seattle, an emergency housing official found that one third to one half of the people needing help were employed, "But the problem will be that they get sick, or their kids get sick, or the family breaks up, and the rent is what goes. So they end up being evicted."

A minimum wage job just won't hack it for the head of a household. Even a $5 an hour job doesn't stretch far enough to cover childcare expenses, rent, utilities, car expenses, and normal household needs. That's why in many of these families, both parents are working. But if, and when, one of them can't, or if the household is headed by a single parent, there just isn't enough money for even substandard living.

A big part of the problem is the lack of low income and affordable housing, an issue that will be discussed at length in another chapter. It's unrealistic to expect that everyone can afford $700 a month rent. There's a reason that low income housing was always needed. When a portion of the labor force is being paid scrawny wages, then at least those wages should be sufficient to cover basic necessities. Affordable housing is the only way to make it possible for these people to live. Unfortunately, in recent years, there has been a decline in affordable housing, and no programs in sight to alleviate the problem.

IT'S REALLY HARD ON THE KIDS

Homelessness is no fun for anyone, but it's especially hard on the children. No home means no fixed address, no identity, no roots. There are many physical, social, and psychological hazards to homeless children. Dr. Ellen Basseek of Harvard found that 47% of these children are slow in their development of either language, physical development, or emotional growth. "This has dire consequences for the future," she said.

> **"THIS HAS DIRE CONSEQUENCES FOR THE FUTURE."**

The health of these children is precarious. Shelter authorities have noticed that the kids often have colds, runny noses, coughs, bronchitis and other chronic health problems. Lack of regular medical attention, lack of vitamin supplements, and lack of regular meals all contribute to this problem.

Majid Ali, a physician's assistant attending homeless children, said, "In the main, we see the same illnesses that we see in the general population, but they are persistent and recurrent among the homeless children in shelters." He noted that there is a lot of upper and lower respiratory infections, head lice, and illnesses related to stress and to living in close quarters. Lack of proper immunizations is common among homeless children.

Hypothermia is another peril to homeless people, and especially for children, since they have a tendency to kick off their blankets even if sleeping outdoors in cool weather. A person can be losing body heat without realizing it, and a child even more so. For instance, a night on the Arizona desert can drop to 40 degrees or lower—much lower than most people expect of such a mild climate. It is very easy in that situation to lose body heat slowly and not realize it's happening.

In January, 1987, Mesa, Arizona mayor Al Brooks asked residents to donate money, food, and blankets to help 150 families who were living in tents northeast of the city. He said, "I have heard of stories of children without shoes and night temperatures severe enough to cause problems."

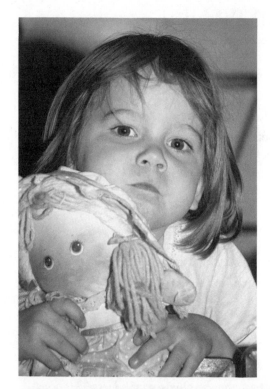

We are seeing
more homeless
children than
ever before.

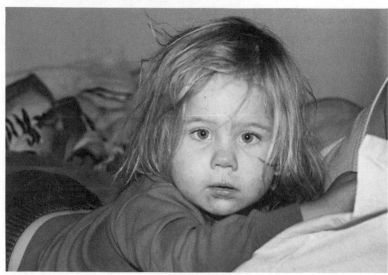

Another Mesa resident, Margie Frost, said, "I was out there last night and saw a 15-month-old baby trying to stay warm."

Health care for homeless people may of necessity become low priority. Parents are looking for work, a way to provide food and shelter, and items like clinic visits become luxuries.

The homeless lifestyle can often lead to social isolation for the child. A home is the basic connection to family, friends, neighborhoods, and schools. Without a home, it's harder for a child to develop certain social skills. Until the family is settled, the child might not attend school for long periods of time. His social life consists of learning to deal with homeless adults or shelter volunteers.

Within the shelters, the social development of the kids is usually even more stunted. Because the parents fear that the children might be abused by other adults, the children are seldom allowed to play alone. Even a simple thing like toilet training may become a major trauma, because there are always other people around. The relationship between the parent and child is there for everyone to see. There is no longer a private relationship. Public parenting puts a strain on both parent and child.

"When you're homeless and you've got children, you feel so terrible inside, so guilty," said one homeless woman. "You look at your kids and they're dirty and there's no place to take a shower."

Homeless parents have little or no control over their lives. The children sense this, and may shift loyalties to those who are providing them with the basic necessities. Confusion over role models may develop, further complicating the child's life. Children also view the aberrant behavior provided by others in a shelter situation, thus leading to their own anti-social behavior. Violence is a problem in and around many shelters, due in part to the extreme amount of stress homelessness provides.

Homeless children are more likely to be abused or neglected, according to a study by the Child Welfare League of America. Ten percent of the children studied were suspected of being abused or neglected. The CWLA director said, "The study supports what many of us in the child welfare field have felt for some time: homelessness is a children's problem."

Homeless children still attending school may become embarrassed about their situation, especially since other children are so quick to tease. Often kids treated like this will become withdrawn, introverted, hostile, bashful, or start misbehaving.Homeless kids may start failing in school. Toddlers may revert to crawling. Other frequent problems cited are bed-wetting, thumb-sucking, nightmares, violent mood swings, suicidal thoughts, abnormal tendencies to be either too aggressive or too withdrawn, and other such stress indicators.

Certain schools will not let homeless children enroll. Rent receipts are often required as proof of residency. A Children's Defense Fund study shows that many schools turn away homeless children when parents cannot prove they live within the district.

Parents may ask their children to lie to their schoolmates about their homelessness, thus creating even more pressure for the child. It's a no-win situation. The youngster is robbed of his childhood. He may even exhibit signs of grieving, because of the loss of his home. Children who are staying in public shelters have problems with the lack of privacy and the confining spaces. Some children blame themselves for the family's homeless situation, feeling that God is punishing the family for something they did wrong.

A child deprived of a home is unable to build upon the security that provides, and it is possible for the pattern to repeat itself in the next generation.

A home is a necessary part of the child's social-psychological development. Unusual and non-traditional homes still contribute to a child's growth. But the lack of a home is severely straining on the life of a youngster.

We as a society owe it to these children to provide them with something as basic as shelter. As one public official asked, "What kind of society is it that doesn't take care of its children?"

"What kind of society is it that doesn't take care of its children?"

PARENTS FEAR AGENCIES WILL TAKE KIDS

One of the things that homeless parents fear most is that homelessness may be grounds for public agencies to take their children away from them. Many parents will stay in cars for weeks rather than ask for help from emergency agencies because of this fear.

There is a basis for this fear. In New Jersey, a priest working with homeless people saw, "The main reason for foster care in New Jersey is homelessness. We are dealing with this problem by splitting up families. It's an evil system."

Not all agencies will split families because of homelessness, but in the past it has been true that homelessness would a the likely cause of placing a child in foster care. The general policy of certain agencies has been the ground rule of "fault", that is, they assumed it was the parent's fault for being homeless, and therefore assumed that the parent was negligent, and therefore believed that they had grounds for splitting the family.

The idea of blaming families for homelessness puts even more strain on these people. They never dreamed of ending up like this. In fact, most of them are truly amazed to find themselves in a homeless situation. "It could never happen to me." But it did.

Agencies that have traditionally served homeless people realize that they lack the expertise and the facilities to deal with families, especially with the complex needs of children. The long-term effect of homelessness can be especially damaging to children.

Homelessness is the ultimate poverty. If for no other reason than for the kids, let's all work to correct this situation. For kids' sakes.

HOMELESSNESS IS THE ULTIMATE POVERTY.

FOR KIDS' SAKES, LET'S DO SOMETHING.

CHAPTER FIVE

AMERICA'S CASTOFFS:
THE MENTALLY ILL HOMELESS

Everything George owns is in a dingy bag with broken handles. He wears old-fashioned brown slacks with no belt and frayed cuffs. His shirt has a small rip across one shoulder. He appears to be about 55-years-old. He has had chronic mental health problems since his youth.

George has been traveling across the country looking for his friend "Charley", who he hasn't seen in 25 years. George doesn't remember Charley's last name or address, but he may live in Seattle now. This type of quest is referred to as "Greyhound therapy" by mental health professionals, as opposed to "three hots and a cot"—institutionalization.

The journey George has undertaken puts him in danger and is of great concern to the mental health worker who has been trying to help him. The problem has been to try to convince George to come into a local clinic for treatment on a voluntary basis. But George has resisted and doesn't even seem to understand what is being suggested. "I've got to go... I've got to go...." George whispered frantically and disappeared off into the night.

Mentally ill people cannot be forced into treatment, even on an outpatient basis. It's part of our "humane system" of mental health care.

THE SYSTEM IS CRAZY

In a dirty Phoenix motel room, a young woman we shall call Stella, squatted for what she thought was a bowel movement—and gave birth to a baby girl. The baby was fine, but Stella suffers from a schizo-affective disorder and probably will for the rest of her life.

Stella occasionally checks into a state psychiatric hospital. She stays long enough to almost become rational. Then she leaves.

She also checks into the county medical hospital once in a while—to give birth. So far she has given birth to four children. And then she wanders the streets again, to get pregnant all over again. Or maybe worse.

Stella's cousin has custody of the children and works vigorously to try to get help for Stella: writing to legislators, social agencies, doctors, lawyers, and law authorities. But to no avail. There is no way to force people to be treated under the current mental health system unless they commit a crime. Then they end up in prison.

Stella's cousin says, "My cousin is mentally ill, but the system that allows all of this to continue—that's crazy."

HOW MANY MENTALLY ILL HOMELESS?

About one third of the homeless population in the United States is mentally ill. That means there may be as many as one million homeless mentally ill persons on the streets of our beloved country. A Ohio study showed that one third of the homeless polled had been in a psychiatric hospital before living on the streets, and half of these had been discharged within the past two years.

The National Institute of Mental Health estimates that 2,400,000 million Americans are chronically mentally ill and that about 1,500,000 of them live in the community. Virtually any one of these persons can be homeless at one time or another.

According to the 1986 US Conference of Mayors survey, an average of 29% of the homeless persons in the survey cities were chronically mentally ill, with numbers ranging from 60% in Louisville, to 45% in Salt Lake City and San Francisco,

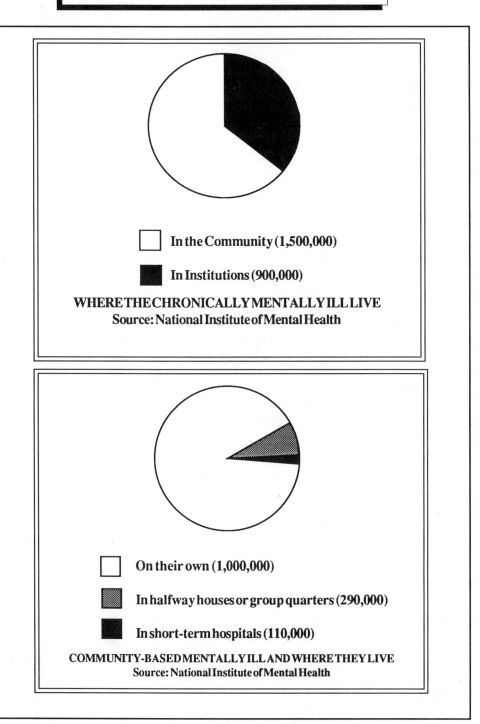

In the Community (1,500,000)

In Institutions (900,000)

WHERE THE CHRONICALLY MENTALLY ILL LIVE
Source: National Institute of Mental Health

On their own (1,000,000)

In halfway houses or group quarters (290,000)

In short-term hospitals (110,000)

COMMUNITY-BASED MENTALLY ILL AND WHERE THEY LIVE
Source: National Institute of Mental Health

40% in Charleston, Minneapolis, Seattle, 15% in Trenton, and 2% in Yonkers.

The report also noted that mental illness combined with the lack of services needed by these people was identified as a major cause of homelessness. The following cities reported:

Nashville: "Lack of suitable living arrangements and services for persons released from mental institutions."

San Francisco: "Mental health treatment monies have never followed the patient released from the state hospitals."

Seattle: "The state's mental health system has forced many chronically ill people into communities where they have a difficult time adjusting to an increasingly competitive job market and stable living conditions."

Charleston: "Lack of transitional housing for mentally ill persons in community."

San Juan (CA): "No adequate mental health facilities in city.

Trenton (NJ): "In most cases the lack of comprehensive support systems for the mentally disabled living in the community has created a new and vulnerable sub-class in many urban neighborhoods."

Why are there so many homeless mentally ill people, and why aren't there services available for them? The blame has been cast on a policy in recent years called "deinstitutionalization."

DEINSTITUTIONALIZATION

The growing demand for civil liberties in the 1960's had an unexpected result: thousands of homeless mentally ill persons in the 1980's. The reforms generated by progressives in the Kennedy administration were meant to be a humane alternative to the unspeakable conditions and abuses found in mental institutions. But the casualties of the plan are numerous.

The reform was labeled "deinstitutionalization", [called sarcastically "dumping" by some] and was the change in policies of who could be admitted to state mental institutions and for how long. Previously, "almost anyone in difficulty who is properly certified" could be committed to a psychiatric hospital. After the reform, only a person who was "a clear danger to himself or to others" could be admitted. A person could be considered "a clear danger" by the courts only if he committed an act of violence. Most state's current laws fall into this category of requiring this "danger standard."

A second group of states allows involuntary commitment if the person is found "gravely disabled—can't attend to the basic needs of food, clothing, and shelter." And the least restrictive laws of all are in Washington, Texas, and Alaska, where a "gravely disabled" person is one who "might have problems in the future" in the areas of attending to their basic needs.

The reform also released hundreds of thousands of patients back to the community. The idea was that the local communities were supposed to provide follow-up care and help the patients adjust to everyday life. The overall goal was to help patients become a productive part of society instead of living in institutions. The idealism was the right of the individual to self-determination and to protect people from possible abuse in institutions. Reformers prided themselves on granting liberty back to the mentally ill.

One of the reasons that reformers and psychiatrists felt that deinstitutionalization would work was the development of powerful "miracle drugs" that could control psychotics—among them Thorazine. These drugs eased bizarre behaviors of some types of mental illnesses and allowed some patients to return home. Others could be treated without long-term hospitalization.

A series of court decisions in the 1960's that intended to protect the mentally ill, gave them greater say in their own care and ordered that treatment be in the least restrictive surroundings as possible and be closer to their homes.

In order to understand why these reforms came about, it is necessary to keep in mind the conditions of long-term psychiatric hospitals in that era. Wretched conditions and overcrowded facilities were the norm. Treatment was often unbearably inhumane. Patients had little opportunity to get well when crowded among wailing, screaming, disoriented people. A real fear among "sane" people was to accidently become admitted to one of these ordeals.

So when civil liberties were being debated in the 1960's, it's no wonder that there was a strong movement towards reform of the mental institutions. That attitude, combined with the knowledge that new psychoactive drugs could help moderate behavior, and with promises that community-based care centers would be built, spurred the reform.

Hospitals released patients by the thousands back to the community. Between 1955 and 1982, the population of mental hospitals dropped from 560,000 to 116,000. During that time, 65% of the liberated patients have achieved tenuous adaptation to community life. Yet thousands of others are on the streets.

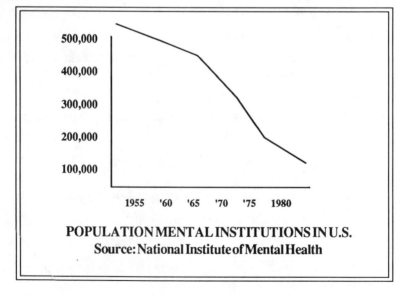

POPULATION MENTAL INSTITUTIONS IN U.S.
Source: National Institute of Mental Health

WHY DID DEINSTITUTIONALIZATION FAIL?

If so many patients have successfully adapted to the community, why are there so many that have ended up homeless? The reason is that the local support organizations failed to materialize as the reformers had anticipated. In 1963, John F. Kennedy signed into legislation a network of community centers to support deinstitutionalized patients. Though 2,000 are needed, only 700 were ever built.

The local safety net that was so crucial to deinstitutionalization hasn't existed. Patients who obtained short-term care in psychiatric hospitals were quickly released—regardless whether there was a facility able to handle follow-up care. So thousands of people have been released to a nonexistent system of community care.

"The idea was that patients would go into the community and be served by community mental health centers...and there would be outpatient support," said John Watson, superintendent of Georgia Regional Hospital, "But it's been the exception rather than the rule."

What happened? The programs were never funded. Local governments became bogged down in controversies over where to locate facilities—neighborhoods fought against having them in their areas. And the mental health system overall is skewed in how the money is appropriated: 70% of state funding for mental health goes to psychiatric hospitals—which care for only 7% of the chronically ill patients. Less than a quarter of the patients discharged from state hospitals have any mental health discharge program.

A typical state mental health budget is:

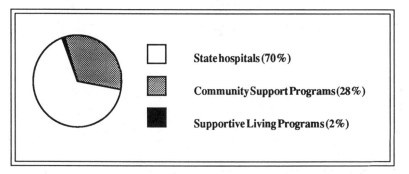

State hospitals (70%)

Community Support Programs (28%)

Supportive Living Programs (2%)

Supportive living programs—such as halfway houses, are especially needed for the chronically ill patients. There are many people who can function in society part of the time, but who need considerable assistance. Living on their own is much too difficult for them, but they do not need the constant supervision of a hospital. Halfway houses are the best alternative for these people, but they're just not available.

Or, as one critic of deinstitutionalization points out, "the money has not followed the patients". As fewer patients were institutionalized, the money remained with the institutions. Although 63% of the nation's chronically ill are at large in the community, two-thirds of the funding still goes to the hospitals.

Thus the mentally ill have kept their right to independence, but have lost urgently needed care. They are ending up wandering aimlessly about the streets. They are, as many mental health care professionals put it, "dying with their rights on."

> **The homeless mentally ill are "dying with their rights on."**

As one psychiatrist said bluntly, "Deinstitutionalization stinks."

HELP IS MORE THAN A PLACE

After looking at the problem of homelessness, mental illness, and the problems caused by deinstitutionalization, Mayor Koch of New York City, in the summer of 1987 called for mentally ill homeless people in the city to be involuntarily hospitalized.

The action was meant to be a solution, but of course it ended up causing more controversy than ever. Joyce Brown was a homeless woman who was committed against her will to a New York City psychiatric hospital shortly after this new policy. She was enraged with the injustice of her predicament, and called the American Civil Liberties Union (ACLU) to help her.

Justice Robert Lippman, in November, 1987, ruled that she be released.

Joyce Brown gained fame over the controversy, and said "They picked on the wrong person, because I'm sane. I'm not insane."

Joyce Brown has become an advocate for the homeless. She now has an apartment, a part-time job, book and movie offers, and has even lectured at Harvard. She advocates better solutions than throwing people into Bellevue Hospital, "We are in dire need of housing. Everyone should take a long, hard took at what's going on in America with homeless on the streets."

What is really needed for these people? Basically, they need a way to keep their dignity and still receive compassionate care.

The American Psychiatric Association's Task Force report "The Homeless Mentally Ill" suggested some solutions:

☆ Establishment of community settings for the mentally ill homeless, ranging from strictly supervised housing where they are constantly monitored, to low-cost housing for those who can live independently.

☆ Creating a case-management system to ensure that each patient has one professional responsible for his care.

"This is no quick fix," noted Dr. John Talbott, one of the researchers on the report.

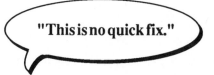

"This is no quick fix."

The mentally ill homeless need a variety of types of housing. For some, they need only low-cost housing with someone to overlook their mental health needs, such as occasional counseling or therapeutic drugs. These persons can manage quite nicely in almost a "normal" lifestyle—holding down a job, doing their own shopping, taking care of their own basic needs—with only minimal help.

Others need various degrees more support. But many are still able to live on their own with help. The most ill of these homeless persons need almost constant care, but are still able to live outside traditional psychiatric hospitals. Different kinds of programs would suit the needs of these people. Some would be similar to halfway houses used for treating alcoholism or parolees. Others could be transitional living programs to ease a person into their own independent home. The most intensive program would be group quarters where constant supervision is available, but yet the people are allowed an amount of freedom so that they could live without excessive restrictions.

An advantage of these programs is that they are much less costly than institutionalization. For instance, it costs $40,000 on the average to keep a person for a year in a psychiatric hospital, but it costs about $6,000 for that person to live in a halfway house. Obviously, the taxpayers still bear the burden, but the burden is truly ours to bear.

A $

B $ $ $ $ $ $ $

A = $6,000 Cost per person at halfway house
B = $40,000 Cost per person at psychiatric hospital

Comparative costs of types of care for the mentally ill

Several model examples exist of fine community mental health programs that keep in mind "helping with compassion yet letting them live with dignity." One example is the Quarterway House in Boston. Another is the Bridge in Chicago.

The Bridge's goal is to be a link to reality for the mentally ill living on their own. The caseworkers work hard to keep their clients out of psychiatric hospitals and to keep them in the community. Nearly all of the patients need some medication to stay on balance. Most of them receive some sort of federal aid.

The caseworkers tend to a variety of needs for their clients—anything from helping them manage their money to helping them learn how to act in social situations. They help buy clothes, food, give them counseling, help them find an apartment—whatever's needed to keep these people from going over the edge. The help given from caseworkers can mean the difference between a functioning individual or one who's facing insurmountable hurdles handling everyday life. The program provides a semblance of normal life for people who might otherwise be sleeping under cardboards in the city park.

The reason that the Bridge program is so successful is not just the philosophy, but because the caseworkers are caring, patient people who offer just the right amount of encouragement and guidance. It's the people who make the difference.

And that's exactly what has to be remembered when solutions are sought for the problems of the mentally ill homeless. It's not just the place that counts, it's the people. Warm, caring, compassionate human beings make the difference.

HELP IS NOT JUST A PLACE, IT'S A PERSON!

**The large number of homeless
runaways is a shocking story.**

CHAPTER SIX

NOBODY'S CHILDREN: HOMELESS RUNAWAYS

Nobody's children. Throwaways. Castoffs. Troubled children. Homeless youth. Runaways. Whatever the label, whatever the reason, the problem is still the same. Young people with nowhere to live and nobody to care for them.

The large number of homeless runaway children is a shocking story. Anywhere from 500,000 to 2,000,000 homeless teens have to face the streets every day in the United States.

A 1983 study by the Department of Health and Human Services found that more than 800,000 children run away from home annually, and that 300,000 children are abandoned each year. That means that the number of children living on their own exceeds one million.

The National Network of Runaway and Youth Services estimates an even higher number. They feel that 1,300,000 to 1,500,000 children are living on the streets, of which one-third are runaways.

About 15,000 homeless youths float through the streets of New York City. In Anchorage, a disturbingly large number of youngsters (1,500) live on the streets at any given time. Probably two hundred of these kids are living in abandoned buildings and crash pads. Other cities have similarly large numbers of homeless runaways.

Comparisons of police reports on runaways show nearly a 50% rise in the number of runaways since 1980. In some areas, the numbers have actually doubled in recent years.

Runaways come from all levels of society. Both boys and girls run away. Girls, however, tend to run away with a friend rather than do it alone. Years ago, it was assumed that only "incorrigibles" ran away from home. That assumption was wrong. It can happen in any family.

IT CAN HAPPEN IN ANY FAMILY.

Three out of five youngsters who make their way to shelters are homeless. "We are seeing fewer kids who have run away on a lark to see the world, and many more kids who have no home to go to," said Martha McDonel of the Youth Haven in Patterson, New Jersey.

A Rutgers University study of teenagers in New Jersey shelters found that:

☆ 30% were runaways
☆ 60% were homeless

A third of these kids had never run away or been homeless before. Unfortunately, that means that two-thirds of them have had recurring problems. And many of the homeless teens never go to shelters because they are afraid of being picked up by authorities, so it's harder to give them aid or to help them reach appropriate service organizations.

The plight of these homeless teens is a crisis that calls for action. "It's absolutely unbelievable this could be taking place. It's a hands-on emergency," said Representative Donald Ferry of Rhode Island.

This is not a romantic Huckleberry Finn situation, where the kids are running to the big city to seek adventure. These are troubled children.

Society has abandoned these runaways. They have nowhere to turn, no home, no work, no way to become involved with the mainstream of this country. They seem like a group that would be more appropriate in Dicken's 19th century London than in contemporary America.

WHO ARE THESE KIDS?

Who are these kids? Why is this happening? What are the kinds of problems that cause teens to end up in the streets?

Let's take a look at some typical runaways.

Elizabeth

Elizabeth is only 16 but she looks much older. Her eyes show nightmarish pain, and a longing for a normal life. The nightmare was not dreamed; it was real. She and her brothers were beaten regularly by their stepfather. He also raped Elizabeth. Not once. But regularly for years.

Elizabeth's mother had temper tantrums. And to top it off, the family was poor. The only light in this young girl's life is her year-old son. She's been in and out of foster homes. She's been thrown out of programs and out of her home. She's lived on the streets. She moved to a nearby state once to live with her father. He moved without telling her.

On the streets she soon sold her body to raise enough money to eat. She became involved in a life that included drugs, alcohol, and abusive men.

Elizabeth feels like she's been thrown away.

Jonah

Jonah's parents divorced when he was 15. They shuttled him back and forth between them. He went to live with a man he thought was a friend, but the man sexually abused him.

Then he tried staying with a friend's parents but was thrown out after an argument. He's now homeless. He's tried several jobs, including being a cook. That job ended in a shouting match. He dropped out of high school. He'd like to become a truck driver or a chef, but he's making no progress towards these goals.

After two years on the streets, Jonah says, "There's a lot of hate in me. I can't trust anyone."

Trish

Trish's mother was only sixteen when she was born, so her grandmother raised her. Later when her mother settled down and had a family, Trish went to live with her. The situation didn't work out. The relationship was distant and tense. Trish had unresolved feelings of rejection and feelings of bitterness towards her mother's other children.

Trish ran away. She doesn't want to go back home, but she has nowhere to turn.

John

Unable to deal with his own homosexuality and not able to confide in his parents, John left home. Confusion over his own sexuality has led him into situations involving male prostitution.

His new "friends" have introduced him to drugs, alcohol, and a lifestyle unfit for a child. Needless to say, the boy is in danger of disease and the possibility of violence.

John has visited counselors who work with runaways, but his visits are irregular and have not resulted in any positive changes for him.

Candy

Candy is sixteen and has several older brothers and sisters. They all left home early without finishing high school. Her parents have been pressuring her to be better than the rest and finish high school and go on to college. She is tired of what she sees as a lack of freedom at home.

Her father drinks a lot and is mean when he's drunk. He once threatened to break both of her arms if she did not do what he told her. Candy is afraid of him.

Her mother is a submissive woman who does not defy her husband in any way, even if he's being abusive. She sulks a lot and seeks revenge in small ways within the family, such as provoking frustrating minor arguments that tend to blow up into major problems.

Candy is a child without proper role models who is being pressured into things she cannot see the value of, at least not by the examples that have been set for her. Her parents' childlike behavior compounds any problems she might have on her own.

Candy is now living on the streets, and has been for several weeks. She lives from day to day, fearing discovery by authorities who might try to send her to a home she detests. She eats irregularly and poorly. She does not often appear at food kitchens because of her determination to remain anonymous, but when she does, she tries to bundle up to look like an older person.

Tom

Tom does not get along with his stepfather. Fresh bruises speak of the abuse he receives at home. He decided he's not going to take it any more. He's tough and determined to make it on his own, but inside he's more than just a little bit afraid.

He has just hitchhiked from Springfield, Massachusetts, to Boston. He would like to stay at his aunt's house, but fears that she will turn him away because of pressures from his parents. She has offered to let him stay before, but his parents refused, saying, "It just wasn't right."

Tom has decided that if his aunt doesn't let him stay, then he will steal a car and head for California, where he feels there's "gold at the end of the rainbow."

BROKEN HOMES OFTEN TO BLAME

What is similar in the stories of most of the runaways today? Generally, these kids come from broken homes, or homes with weak family relationships. "Almost 90% of our kids are from broken homes," said Carolyn Collins, a counselor at Sojourn House, a temporary group counseling home for teenagers in Mobile, Alabama."And we are getting more and more kids that have been sexually abused."

"Almost 90% of our kids are from broken homes."

95

Often the divorced parents are shuttling the child back and forth and back and forth until the child feels rejected by both of them. Stepfathers, stepmothers, halfbrothers, halfsisters, and all sorts of complicated relationships can add tension to the family situation. Sometimes the kids aren't quite sure where they fit in, and sometimes they don't feel that they fit in at all.

That's not to say that there is only one type of "family" that is acceptable. We all realize that many sorts of families can work, but it's the ones that aren't working out that are a source of problems for children. And these problems can result in runaway homeless kids.

Yet there's no one single reason that kids runaway. Besides tense family relationships, there's also sexual and physical abuse, often by parents who have not grown up themselves. Alcohol, drugs, and finances are often contributing factors to the reasons the kids are mistreated.

Mistreatment causes children to feel that they aren't wanted. Perhaps some parents never wanted the kids in the first place, judging by how much abuse they inflict on them. Childhood has been idealized as a happy time, full of fantasy and laughter. But for many kids, that simply is not so. "A lot of children out there lead very unhappy lives. Many are happier in the street than they are in their own homes," stated a Michigan police officer.

In some families, the parents and children simply do not communicate. Parents may be pressuring their children to do better in school, or to choose a career that the parents want. Rules that parents apply may seem harsh to the kids. Perhaps the parents don't explain the reasons for their rules or don't even find time to spend with their children.

When the child finally leaves, the parents exclaim, "Things weren't that bad!" But obviously if everything had been rosy, the child would not have left.

When family pressures mount, the children may end up in foster homes until the situation cools off. When this happens, the child may end up more confused than ever. Is he wanted? Or is he just a pet to be shuttled around when it's convenient?

Family problems are the
main reasons kids run away.

There are times that a foster home can be very helpful for temporary difficulties, but when the problem lies in the basic relationships of the family, the foster home is only a calm between storms.

Other factors can influence a teenager to runaway. Kids involved with alcohol and drugs may not feel that they have anyone to turn to at home. Or they may become withdrawn and not even try to respond to help that parents offer. Pregnancies often frighten girls enough to run away. Some fear that their parents would never understand; others are ashamed and don't want to disappoint their parents.

Not wanting to disappoint parents can play a factor in some kid's reasons to leave home. Children may be overwhelmed by their sexual awakening, especially if they feel that they are homosexual. They aren't always sure that their parents will accept them. Others are afraid that they won't be able to live up to their parents' high standards in other ways, such as academics, or career choices.

Some children are just starved for attention. Parents who are workaholics aren't spending time with the most important people in their lives—their kids. These parents may be providing the best material things available—the best homes, the best clothes, the best cars, the best clubs, the best food. But they are forgetting that spending time together, showing affection, and learning about each other, are the most important parts of life.

The 1987 Rutgers University study of homeless kids found that :

☆ 61% of the families had conflicts
☆ 30% of the families had divorce problems
☆ 27% of the families had alcohol and drug abuse problems
☆ 22% of the families had health or mental problems
☆ 19% of the families had problems with violence
☆ 18% of the families had financial problems.

Obviously, some of the families had multiple problems.

One of the most shocking reasons that children are homeless is because of abandonment. To think that 300,000 to 500,000 children are abandoned each year! The thought that parents would abandon children is disturbing enough, but the large

300,000 to 500,000 children are abandoned each year!

numbers of people doing so is profoundly alarming. There used to be a joke used by comedians about when they were kids they came home one day and their parents had moved. It was so unbelievable that anyone would do such a thing, that it seemed funny. But to actually have this happen is not funny at all! What type of people would actually leave their children defenseless, homeless, and alone? Only the most despicable person on earth would ever abandon a child.

Occasionally the family life has nothing whatsoever to do with the child leaving home. The child may just wish for total freedom, to "hit the road and see what life is all about". He may want to grow up right away instead of waiting around and living under his parents' roof. It's his ultimate expression of rebellion, of cutting the parental apron strings.

Other kids are going through a painful and lonely time of change—the difficult transformation from child to adult. They are trying to break with their past (their childhood) in order to become adults. Inside a teenager is a bundle of feelings that isn't always obvious on the outside. They are searching hard to figure out who they are, trying to clarify their role as people, and some feel the need to leave home to do it.

But these kids are in the minority. Basically, it's poor family relationships that cause kids to become runaways. In almost every case of runaway children, the trouble can be traced to family problems. The disturbing pressures of unstable family relationships, a consistent environment of hostility or tension, shallow interactions between family members, combined with possible physical, mental and sexual abuse, are the root of the problem.

Neglect, abuse, rejection, loneliness, lack of communication. These are the seeds of runaways.

Running away is a strong statement. It is almost always an expression of the child's pain or conflicting emotions. It's a telegram saying, "I just can't deal with this any more." Or, "Please help me." It's not an act that a child consciously chooses, it's an act he is forced into.

Counselors now feel that childhood running away may be a sign of a strong person, because at least that child is making a strong effort to change things that are wrong. The action is a safety valve on inner pressures. The child is at least trying to escape from abuse or turmoil. However, it's a drastic step, and one that may harm the child in the long run.

Running away is saying,
"Please help me!"

LIFE IN THE STREETS IS NOT ALL IT'S CRACKED UP TO BE

Prostitution. Drugs. Alcohol. Stealing. Malnutrition. Hypothermia.

Is this any way for a kid to live?

But how many kids have a choice once they're homeless and destitute? Frankly, they don't make plans to run away. They just do it. Zip! And they're gone.

They usually leave home with no resources nor far-sighted plans. Sometimes they think they will go live with a friend, but often that only lasts a day or two. Sooner or later they end up on the streets.

How do they survive? Very few seek shelters or help from social organizations. They usually don't have money for a motel, and even if they do, motels are leery of harboring runaways. They survive one day at a time. They adapt. They get tough, cynical, amoral, manipulative.

Keep in mind the child labor laws. They can't just go out and get a job if they are under age. They need special permits signed by their parents for that. Panhandling isn't as often viewed as an alternative. So how do they get money?

They turn to stealing or prostitution. They learn to shoplift to eat. Both boys and girls turn to prostitution. Street boys make their living hustling sex to gay or bisexual men. Girls sell their bodies in order to be able to eat. Some end up with pimps; others work alone. They learn to trade their bodies for a warm place to sleep. They sleep in a different bed every night with different people. They have no idea what the morning will bring.

Some steal, some run drugs for dealers, some cash stolen checks or return shoplifted goods for cash. They are exploited by adults who turn them into con-artists. They learn to be street-wise and tough. They are forced to break the law to survive.

Invariably, they get hooked into the drug scene. Alcohol and drugs help them get through the day, but ruin their bodies and minds.

They are subject to violence: rape, beatings, even murder. Thirteen-year-old Mary Frances Harvey was shot to death in 1980, and untold more have died at the hands of brutal adults. Hitchhiking is another risky proposition that runaways invariably try.

The sex and drugs open the way for diseases, especially AIDS. They are subject to death by overdose. Poor nutrition compounds health problems. One girl told of eating candy bars and pretzels to survive. Others had to raid garbage cans for scraps. Girls often become pregnant; some resort to unclean backroom or self-inflicted abortions.

Their clothing is inadequate, and during the winter months they suffer from hypothermia. They live in crash pads or in abandoned buildings. Trying to keep warm can cause other problems. In Michigan two fifteen-year-old runaway girls were found asphyxiated by a small charcoal heater they were using to keep warm in an empty house.

These kids have mental and social problems related to their lifestyle as well. They are manipulative, but untrusting. They can't relate to other people. Their ability to socialize stagnates. Some develop serious mental health problems and are unable to cope with life. Some become suicidal. One girl said, "God must not want me to live."

One girl said, "God must not want me to live."

Others develop habits that will eventually permanently damage their lives and lead them into a criminal lifestyle forever. If society does not deal successfully with these youngsters when they first need help, then it will surely have to deal with them later—as criminals, as permanently unskilled and unemployable, as mental health patients, or as parents who perpetuate these problems in their own children.

Unfortunately, as Father Bruce Ritter says in *Covenant House*, most will not find a way out. He said "Kids don't survive very long on the street—at least in any recognizably human way. The distortion of the personality, the erosion of character are swift and massive and almost always irreversible." They need to be reached quickly, for after one year on the streets, many have committed suicide, been murdered, or overdosed on drugs.

Most of these kids were running away from something terrible. But, "So many times the things you encounter are even worse than what you're running from," said John Hart, a counselor at Threshold Youth Services in Sioux Falls, South Dakota.

The physical, mental, and social dangers to these homeless runaways are enormous. We cannot and should not allow this to happen to our future leaders.

THE LAW AND RUNAWAYS

In most states, runaways are no longer locked up by the police. In past years, running away was considered a criminal offense, for which children could be incarcerated. A reform took place which decriminalized runaways. By 1985, all but five states had adopted laws against locking up "status offenders", those offenses being running away, drinking, and incorrigibility. Status offenses are ones that are illegal only because of the age of the offender. The five states that still allow these children to be locked up are South Dakota, North Dakota, Wyoming, Hawaii, and Nevada.

One of the people promoting this reform was Ira Schwartz, who in 1979-1980 was in charge of the Office of Juvenile Justice and Delinquency Prevention under Jimmy Carter. He cited many reasons for not locking up status offenders, and stated, "These kids largely are not thugs and hoods and heavy criminals. They ought not be locked up with thugs and crooks."

The reform was spearheaded by the Juvenile Justice and Delinquency

Prevention Control Act of 1974 that required states that wanted federal delinquency program grants to forbid incarceration of status offenders.

Police agencies around the nation differ in their new approach to runaways, but many follow the same guidelines as the Grand Rapids, Michigan, police force. In that city, the police have three choices when they round up runaways that are not suspected of any crime: take them home, take them to the Juvenile Court system's Crisis Intervention Center, or take them to The Bridge, a shelter for runaways.

Running away used to be viewed as a crime, but now is seen as children trying to find a healthy solution for an unhealthy situation. However, unless these runaways find appropriate help fast after leaving home, their life will turn into an even unhealthier situation.

What is it that these kids need? What are appropriate solutions to the problem?

Most psychologists agree that runaways need counseling. The kids also need a secure, warm (both physically and emotionally) environment, food, and possibly job training. Their first needs are physical—shelter and food. Then they need a plan for the future, whether that be permanent group housing, foster care, return to home, apartment placement, job training, or schooling. Their emotional and social needs also need to be dealt with. The following sections will show how agencies are trying to deal with these needs, and whether or not the needs are being met.

AGENCIES, SHELTERS, & RUNAWAYS

One place for runaways is within the shelter system. However, these shelters are inadequate. For one thing, there isn't enough shelters now for all of the homeless people in America. So many of them do not get a roof over their heads at night already, so it would be impossible to expect that there is space for every teenage runaway.

The other inadequacy is that a shelter is a roof and walls only, not direction for people's lives. Teenagers especially need much more. They need counseling, protection, job training, and someone to motivate and direct them.

In some states, shelters refer runaways to other social agencies within the city, such as Child Protection Services or the Department for Children and Their Families (DCF), or to independent services, such as Covenant House (which will be discussed later in detail.) Except for Covenant House, these services are also usually inadequate for dealing with all of the needs of the child.

Social agencies' usual answer to the problem is to try to find foster care for the child, which often does not solve the original problems or create new direction for the child. Foster care can best be described as a stepping-stone solution, because what often happens is that these children go from one foster home to another to another, often running away repeatedly. They are then looked upon as incorrigibles instead of receiving the care they so desperately need.

To be quite fair, most of these state social agencies are already overburdened. The social workers have excessive caseloads, and there is not enough foster homes available. There are programs called early-intervention programs, which are designed to intercede before the child runs away, to help solve problems before they become unbearable. But quite frankly, these programs are underfunded. There are just not enough good programs and enough money appropriated to help these needy teens.

Occasionally there are shelters just for runaways. Some are considered quite a haven for kids; others not so glorious. Regardless of how comfortable or uncomfortable these teen shelters are, there do not seem to be enough of them.

In New Jersey, for instance, there are 6 shelters for kids—four for boys, two for girls. All are privately run by contracts to the Department of Children and Their Families (DCF). All are in cities, with four of them in low-income neighborhoods.

The conditions within these shelters varies. At the West Warwick, New Jersey, shelter and at the Providence, New Jersey, shelter, the environment is clean. There is qualified counseling available.

The other shelters are not so fine. The others are in need of extensive repairs—the paint is peeling off the ceilings, furniture is broken, mattresses are ripped, and showers have been destroyed. Very little, if any, counseling is available in these shelters. Most of the children of school-age in these inadequate shelters are not attending school—a very hypocritical message in this day and age of compulsory attendance laws. It says to the kids, "Hey, kids with parents and a decent home deserve and education and a place in this world, but the rest of you don't deserve even a clean place to sleep."

Most states are in the same predicament. In Rhode Island, there are also 6 teen shelters. These are also run privately under contract to DCF. But programs to help these teens are grossly inadequate and underfunded. "We don't have anything to offer these kids. We have not provided a place where they feel comfortable, secure, where they can say, 'Yes, I am wanted here,'" said Representative Donald Ferry, who is Chairman of the Rhode Island House Finance Committee subcommittee on DCF.

Altogether too many cities are like Minneapolis, in which there are no teen shelters at all. Teenagers are not even allowed in shelters for homeless adults in Minneapolis. The plight of runaways in cities such as this is a dire predicament—they can't go home for various reasons, the streets are dangerous, yet no one else wants them either.

Some states have slightly better facilities. In Grand Rapids, Michigan, there is a teen shelter called The Bridge. The Bridge is part of the Kent County, Michigan, juvenile court system. This shelter has a homey atmosphere with a recreation/living room full of overstuffed couches and a pool table. Rules are strict, but fair. Chores are assigned for infringement of rules. Counseling is available. However, there are only 13 beds available at The Bridge.

The Relatives is a shelter in Charlotte, North Carolina, with a good reputation for a clean environment and counseling for the kids. This shelter is funded by public grants and private donations. However, once again there are only a few beds: 9 in all.

Inadequate facilities cannot help the millions of kids with serious problems. These kids need more and better programs so that they need not end up homeless and hopeless.

> Kids need a place where they can say, "I am wanted here."

PROJECT SAFE PLACE

There are special programs being designed for teenage runaways and their special needs. The ones discussed here are "Project Safe Place" (national), "Home Free" (national) and the very special project of Covenant House (national).

Country singer Larry Gatlin's recent single and video *Runaway Go Home* were a part of the nationwide Project Safe Place for runaway teenagers. The video features four kids talking about the dangers they faced when they ran away. This project wants to inform kids about the many dangers there are and to let them know that sometimes what they find when they runaway is worse than what they ran from.

The project is federally funded and has received cooperation from various local agencies. In Los Angeles, County Supervisor Deane Dana joined forces with Larry Gatlin to help the project. Decals were placed in local participating businesses to help guide children who may need the help. A great benefit of this program is that it is operated with the voluntary cooperation of local businesses and county shelters, saving the taxpayers much money. Larry Gatlin contributed the song and video after becoming concerned over the plight of runaways when he noticed a Continental Trailways billboard in Illinois offering a free ride home for runaways.

In Los Angeles, businesses will be designated "Safe Places" and employees at these designated "Safe Places" will be trained to spot the children who need help and to guide them to appropriate facilities. The businesses will contact the local shelters, which in turn will help the children.

The beauty of this program is obvious. It's people helping people. It's not just a bureaucratic solution overburdening an already overworked social agency. Instead, it's people who see a need and lend a hand. They are saying, in effect, "We **can** make a difference."

**The beauty of this program is obvious.
It's people helping people.**

HOME FREE

Richard Voorhees, a New Jersey police captain and the father of three children, was named the "Police Officer of the Year" in 1985 by the International Association of Chiefs of Police (IACP) for his work with runaways and for conceiving and promoting the "Home-Free" project.

Voorhees' story is a compelling one. One day in midwinter 1984, he attended a seminar about missing and runaway children. The guest speaker was John Walsh, father of Adam Walsh, the 6-year-old child who was kidnapped and murdered at a shopping mall in south Florida. Walsh's activities with the National Center for Missing and Exploited Children have been the vehicle propelling national attention on these abused children.

Voorhees recalls that day when he heard Walsh speak. "He really blasted the police that day," he said. "He argued that we were not doing enough, that we seemed more concerned with stolen cars. That was his message. It was so strong that when it was over, I felt guilty."

The guilt feeling reminded him of a certain evening ten years earlier when he received a teary call from a fourteen-year-old runaway girl. The girl had runaway from her parents in New Jersey because of serious family problems. Her dad drank and was abusive. She had hitchhiked all of the way to Florida, and was broke. She tried calling her parents collect, but they refused the call. Then she did the thing that changed the lives of so many other runaways. She called Richard Voorhees.

Voorhees said that the only thing he could do is to wire her money. He sent $100 to a Florida police station so that the child could have enough money for a bus ticket home. The Florida police found the girl a place to stay in a local shelter until she returned home by bus three days later.

The memory of that incident, and the guilty feeling that Walsh incited, prodded Voorhees to action. On the night of the lecture, February 29, 1984, he wrote a letter to the Greyhound bus company. He suggested that every runaway be provided a free ride home via bus, regardless of where they lived.

Greyhound replied that it was not interested in the idea because a free ride might provoke some teenagers into running away. The company official pointed out

Chief Richard Voorhees, founder of Home Free
Photo: Courtesy of Richard Voorhees

that Greyhound had always tried to provide shelter information for runaways. Their policy, instituted in 1979, was to have posters in their terminals that read "Don't Rely on Strangers." There were brochures available that listed various agencies that would help a runaway. Terminal personnel actively helped runaways get in touch with their families to make arrangements to return home. About 350,000 of these cards a year are distributed. For the time being, the company's official policy was to remain the same.

Although disappointed, Voorhees tried again. He mailed the same suggestion to Continental Trailways bus company. Soon a company official was telephoning him, ecstatic over the idea, and wanting to know how to make it work.

The main question they needed to work out was—how could the bus company confirm that the children were indeed runaways? Voorhees suggested that they keep the plan as simple as possible, both to help the runaways and also to encourage local police officers to use the program. Simplicity was the key.

Voorhees took one more very important step. He put together the bus company officials and the president of the International Association of Chiefs of Police. From their discussions emerged the guidelines for "Home Free". The simple, yet effective, policy would be:

1. Any youngster 18 years or younger would be eligible.
2. The youngster or the Trailways clerk must notify local police to verify that the child was listed as missing on the national computer.
3. The parents of the child must be notified which bus their child would be riding.
4. A police officer would accompany the child to the bus depot.
5. The trip home would be voluntary on the part of the child.

Operation: Home Free began on June 7, 1984.

As Paul Harvey might say, "Now for the rest of the story." About the same time that Voorhees was working with Trailways, Greyhound was working with the National Center for Missing and Exploited Children in Washington, DC. Greyhound began a program called "Let's Find 'Em—Missing Children & Their Families".This program helps families become reunited with their missing children, such as the ones you see on milk cartons. In the case of kidnapped children, the parents may be eligible for free transportation by the bus company so that they can pick up their kids.The bus company works hand in hand with the National Center for Missing and Exploited Children in Washington DC (1-800-843-5678).

In August of 1987, the Greyhound bus company acquired the Trailways lines. Although there are still terminals named "Trailways" and you can still call a Trailways phone number for tickets, the company is now owned by Greyhound. When the companies became one, the company officials decided to keep both "Operation: Home Free" and "Let's Find 'Em". As a customer service representative said, "Both programs had value, so it was decided not to drop either one." An official policy was issued September 11, 1987. More information can be obtained through the customer service department of Greyhound in Dallas at 214-744-6509.

Thousands of runaways have been provided with a ride home through this incredible, yet simple program. It's another example of how something people-to-people works so well. And it was all because one person cared enough to write a letter.

One person can make a difference!

COVENANT HOUSE

Covenant House was founded in 1972 in New York City by Father Bruce Ritter, a Catholic priest who saw the desperate need for something special for runaways. He was concerned about the runaways who turned to drugs and prostitution to survive. Before opening Covenant House, he used to shelter these kids at his own apartment.

Now there are four Covenant Houses in the United States: New York, Fort Lauderdale, Houston, and Anchorage. There is another in Toronto, Canada, one in Guatemala and one in Panama. More are planned for New Orleans and other cities.

Covenant House has grown from one man's concern into several permanent shelters, but it's more than just that. Because of media attention, like ABC's News Nightline, September 29, 1987, "The Story Never Goes Away" with Ted Koppel on homeless youths with Father Ritter, and the book *Covenant House,* the concept is now a national effort to help runaways. There is a toll-free hotline number 1-800-999-9999 that is available for teens to help them get home or to help them seek assistance wherever they are.

The shelters provide regular hot meals, a clean place to sleep, and counseling. A Covenant House spokesman says that about 38% of the children are reunited with their families, enter a drug or alcohol rehabilitation program, or learn to support themselves. Each child who stays at the shelter must agree to help form an individual plan for their future, whether that be going back to their families, getting a job, or other plans. They must work towards their individual plan, and if they violate

Father Bruce Ritter, founder of Covenant House
Photo: Courtesy of Covenant House

it, they may be asked to leave the shelter. With children under the age of 18, the success rate (determined by the child reaching his plan's goals) is 60%.

The organization now has a program called Rites of Passage, which with the help of seven Wall Street businessmen, provides career guidance for some of the kids. They are required to submit to testing and a series of interviews. Rites of Passage will also help the kids apply for college. Covenant House has a scholarship fund available to any resident who qualifies for college enrollment.

Another advantage of these shelters is that health care is provided. A clinic is on the premises, staffed with nurses and often a physician who is volunteering his/her services. Young mothers and pregnant girls are given the medical attention they need.

Covenant House receives only 5% state and federal funds. It accepts youths up to the age of 21. Its success is largely dependent on the personalized care that the runaways receive. "We don't try to preach to the kids," said Paula Tibbets, of the Fort Lauderdale facility.

The Fort Lauderdale facility was the result of several local people contacting Father Ritter independently because of the growing number of homeless children on the "Strip", Fort Lauderdale's beachfront area. The group included a circuit judge, a radio station president, and a former Junior League president. These people decided to get involved in the effort to open a Ft. Lauderdale shelter. The Sandcastle Motel at 733 Breakers Avenue, one block from the Strip, was purchased and renovated so that it now has 88 beds.

Once again—one person can make a difference!

ONE PERSON CAN MAKE A DIFFERENCE!

All of these fine examples prove how one person who cares, and tries, can make a mighty difference. Larry Gatlin, Richard Voorhees, Father Ritter, and you!

In spite of these great programs, there is more to be done. There is still a great need for help for runaways. There are not nearly enough shelters nor enough volunteers to help these homeless youths. The dangers to these children are enormous, the need is still immense.

To find out how you can help, contact Covenant House or your local shelters. Important phone numbers follow.

IMPORTANT PHONE NUMBERS

Covenant House toll-free national hotline
1-800-999-9999

National Center for Missing/Exploited Children
1-800-843-5678

Greyhound customer service (Dallas)
214-744-6509

DELIVERY --
12th Ave Door

ATTENTION
RUNAWAYS!

FOR HELP CALL
1-800-999-9999

Anywhere in the US

Photo: © Jodi Abodeely 1988
All rights reserved.

CHAPTER SEVEN:

WHO'S POISONING THE FOOD?
THE RISKS OF BEING HOMELESS

From poisoned food in dumpsters to beatings from blanket thieves; from trembling hands to tuberculosis; from freezing to death while sleeping to the feelings of overwhelming despair; from discouragement to death—these are just a few of the risks of being homeless.

Some of the problems faced by homeless people might be obvious, such as lack of shelter, lack of food, or improper clothing. But these people face many many more perils daily than what is even imaginable. The physical, mental, and social hazards are tremendous. Few people survive very long on the streets.

"OUR RESTROOMS ARE FOR CUSTOMERS ONLY!"

The lack of public restroom facilities is bad enough for most people, especially tourists, but when you have no home, it's profoundly irritating. Few cities have installed municipal facilities, except sometimes in parks. Private businesses are not welcoming to the use of their restrooms by homeless people. It's a problem that most people wouldn't even think of, but one that is encountered daily by homeless people.

The lack of public restrooms is only a minor inconvenience to homeless people compared to the other physical risks they face everyday. Lack of sleep can cause numerous problems, apparent in aching bodies, throbbing heads, and trembling hands. Some people think that these symptoms are only from alcohol and drug addiction, but try sleeping outside in mid-winter temperatures for a couple of nights. You'd have an aching body, a throbbing head, and trembling hands too. And perhaps you'd reach for a bottle to warm yourself also.

Alcohol and drug abuse are a big problem among a segment of the homeless people, especially the single persons. It's not always a clear case of them being homeless because their addiction caused their problems. Sometimes it's a question of which came first, the chicken or the egg? Are they homeless because they have these problems, or do they have these problems because they are homeless?

Malnutrition is common among homeless people. Sometimes they are able to receive occasional meals from food services, but that's not always possible, depending on where they are. If they have any money at all, they may eat sporadically, or without proper nutritional requirements. Some homeless runaways have told of surviving on candy bars and potato chips—not a healthy combination in the long run.

Hunger can cause problems of its own. A very hungry person may do almost anything to get something to eat, such as "dumpster-diving". That's the practice of crawling into garbage bins to find discarded food. That's a dangerous way to eat, especially considering the hazards. Disease and chemical poisoning are always a possibility.

But worse than that—some people have actually poisoned the food in their dumpsters to prevent hungry people from eating there. A health official in Columbus, Ohio, said, "In Orlando, a guy told me he sprays the food in his dumpster with bleach or bug spray, anything to keep these guys from eating it. If they know they'll get sick, they'll go somewhere else."

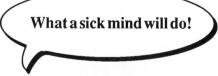

What a sick mind will do!

Malnutrition is especially threatening for children. It stunts their physical and intellectual growth. A well-balanced diet is something no child should have to be denied, for any reason.

Lice is common among homeless people because of where they have to sleep. It's not unusual to see the arms of homeless people covered by scabs from ants that bite them in their sleep. Outdoor living might seem romantic to tenters, but as a constant lifestyle, it causes people to live side-by-side with bugs, rodents, and things that cause disease and skin problems.

Since proper medical care cannot be a priority for a person who doesn't even have a home, other medical problems occur. One man in a Norfolk, Virginia, shelter had diabetes, and wasn't taking his insulin. When asked why, he said that, "You just give up. You can't take it any more."

Homeless people are afflicted with a great number of maladies. A study of medical treatment for the homeless found these statistics:

☆ 16.4% had upper respiratory infections
☆ 9.5% had injuries and poisonings
☆ 8.4% had problems with the nervous system
☆ 8.2% had skin disorders
☆ 7.9% had problems with their circulatory system
☆ 6% had problems with their digestive system

Tuberculosis has been found in a higher rate among homeless populations than among the rest of the nation. Since 1984, three outbreaks of tuberculosis in shelters for the homeless have been reported to the Center for Disease Control in Atlanta. Studies have found that 1.6% to 6.8% of homeless people have clinically active tuberculosis. This is 150 to 300 times higher than the nationwide rate. Crowding and poor ventilation within shelters is blamed for this condition.

VIOLENCE AND DEATH A CONSTANT THREAT

Poor medical treatment is only part of the risk of being homeless. One thing a homeless person learns right away is that he will live constantly under the threat of violence and even death.

Blanket thieves prey among the weaker of the homeless persons. Sometimes groups of homeless people band together to protect themselves from those who would steal from them while they're sleeping. One man said that blanket thieves are like "vultures up and down the streets at night." Beatings and robberies are common.

Death is something you learn to live with if you're homeless. It's not something that just happens to people down the street or to "them". It's real and it's with you all the time. "People are dying," said a 7-year-old living in a hotel provided for the homeless in New York City. "Some are good and they're still dying."

> **"Blanket thieves are like vultures up and down the streets at night."**

Hypothermia is a constant threat when you're sleeping without a shelter. Many people have frozen to death, even in places you'd consider to be moderate climates. That's because a moderate climate can be deceiving. Even the desert of Arizona can drop to freezing at night during the winter months.

And of course, there's suicide. In a transient encampment near Pompano Beach, Florida, at least six (and maybe nine) homeless people have committed suicide by sitting on the railroad tracks in front of an approaching train. First there was Jack, who had lost his job, his girlfriend, and his home. Then there was Steve, who was only a kid, probably a runaway. Then Dave, and Bob, and Annie, and Bobby.

Just look at some of the recent reports on the deaths of homeless people:

☆ *Philadelphia Inquirer,* February 1, 1987, "42 City Homeless Die in 2 years", homeless persons died from exposure,
violent crime, accidents, and untreated illnesses. That's about
two a month.

☆ *Tempe (AZ) Tribune,* November 7, 1987, "Report:
Lot of Homeless Dead", at least 121 homeless persons
died in Maricopa County, Arizona, over a period of one
year. Two were under the age of 19, 30 were between the
ages of 20 and 39, 14 were between the ages of 40 and 49,
56 were between the ages of 50 and 69, and the rest older or
unknown.

☆ *Los Angeles Herald Examiner,* January 18, 1987, "Two Die in Cold on L.A.'s Streets". Two homeless die from near-freezing temperatures.

☆ *Los Angeles Daily News,* January 22,1987, "City Building OK'd as Homeless Shelter". Same week as above, but four homeless people froze to death in Los Angeles that weekend.

☆ *Anchorage Daily News,* November 10, 1986, "Cold Alert System Instituted". About death of Francis Trader who froze to death the year before.

☆ *San Francisco Examiner,* September 19, 1986, "Activists Seek Funding to Shelter Berkeley's Homeless", telling about four homeless men who died due to a fire in an abandoned building.

☆ *Jacksonville (FL) Times-Union,* January 28, 1986, "City Shelters Overflow", homeless Carl Schossler died of exposure.

☆ *Kansas City (MO) Times,* April 5, 1986, "Funeral for an 'Invisible Friend' ", about the murder of homeless Mrs. Taylor.

And the list of death reports of homeless people goes on and on like a bad dream.

"I DON'T WANT TO FEEL THIS BAD"

The physical dangers of being homeless are bad enough. But compounded with those problems are the mental and emotional dangers of the situation. Feelings of worthlessness, despair, hopelessness, and self-doubt add to the anxieties of people without permanent shelter.

Not knowing where your next meal is coming from, or whether you'll be warm enough tonight, can be extremely stressful. It leads to an inability to concentrate on anything but basic needs. When people complain about homeless people and say, "Why don't they just get a job?" they are forgetting the nature of homelessness. It becomes an emotional condition as well as a physical one.

A person who becomes homeless through a series of misfortunes, even if some of them are partly of his own fault, would still like to maintain a "sense of mastery" over his own life, and over his own abilities. That is, he would still like to believe that he can achieve success in his life. But the realities of homelessness soon distort this normal picture of what life is all about. Soon life is viewed no farther than the next meal or a place to sit in the sun.

The sense of loneliness felt by the homeless has been expressed by George Harvey's poem. George was living on the streets of Tucson when he wrote:

> While I was walking on a street I did not know,
> looking for someone to talk to, something to do
> that would show my spirits were down, they
> dragged on the ground, my clothes were nothing
> but rags, my eyes, blood-shot, tired and sagged,
> rolled up on dark-colored bags.
> My feet were all blisters, my legs all bone.
> I walked and walked all alone.

COMFORTING THE HOMELESS.

Photo: Suzanne Starr, 3/19/87
Reprinted with permission of *The Arizona Republic.*
Permission does not imply endorsement by the newspaper.

When a person does get a chance to follow up on a lead for a job interview, things don't always work out because the most minor problem can be a major interference if you're homeless. Sometimes it's as simple as finding bus fare to a job interview or the money to buy the proper clothing for a job.

Roy Moore of Tennessee had a chance for a job that required a $22 pair of boots—but he didn't have the $22.

Donald Emerson of Indiana said that he had an interview for a nurse's aide job, but he didn't have bus fare to get there. So he walked for two and a half hours to get there, and two and a half hours to get back. And he didn't get the job. He said, "I think to myself, 'Oh well, I didn't get the job today, maybe tomorrow.' Then I think, why bother?"

Discouragement sets in. Despair follows like a nasty bedfellow.

People who are trying to get out of the situation of hopelessness get tired of hearing "You can't." Despair can lead to anger, but anger to nowhere. Rejection is a fact of life, but seems overpowering when you're homeless.

Being homeless can also mean a greater risk of mental illness. As pointed out in an earlier chapter, a great many of today's homeless are the deinstitutionalized mentally ill persons. But aside from those people, the chance of developing mental illnesses if you are poor, and especially if you are homeless, are 40% greater than for persons living in the highest social class in this nation (as shown in a Cornell study). Several other studies have back up this conclusion, saying that the poor are subject to more mental illnesses than anyone else in the society, and that their disturbances tend to be more serious than those of any other class.

And even for those homeless persons who do not develop severe mental illnesses, there can often be long-term emotional problems because of homelessness. Behavioral problems can become ingrained; anti-social attitudes can become a part of their life. Through rejection and despair, they may become mistrustful of other people for the rest of their life.

"WHY CAN'T I VOTE?"

A homeless person is often denied basic constitutional rights simply on the basis of his homelessness. Imagine not being able to get a driver's license or a library card because you have no address. Imagine trying to fill out a job application with no phone number, and only the address of a Salvation Army shelter as your permanent address. How could you even get a welfare check or food stamps so that you could begin again, if you have no address?

It's a terrible Catch-22 effect in this country that you have to have an address to be "real".

> **Without an address, you are not really a citizen, not really employable, not able to drive, not able to be anybody.**

In 1986, a homeless man in Colorado sued the state for the right to vote. Within the past years, similar cases concerning "permanent residence" clauses have been put the test in New York, the District of Columbia, Pennsylvania, and California.

Street people have begun to plead for their basic rights as citizens and as human beings. Recently a homeless coalition in Tennessee asked that they be treated humanely on the issues of:

✔ Medical care.
✔ Employment and housing opportunities.
✔ Transportation to reach places of need.
✔ Police harassment.

They were asking for compassion for basic human rights. One member said, "We don't feel like our rights should be denied because we live on the streets."

Other problems of being homelessness are not always so apparent, such as lack of access to what's happening in the world, or even in the neighborhood. Homeless people have no TV, no newspapers—at least not on a regular basis. Things like this that keep a person informed, and part of the world, are hard to come by when you don't even know where you'll be sleeping tonight.

Family abuse occurs more frequently in families under stress, and is apparent in some cases of homeless families. The children already have plenty to deal with, and adding the burden of verbal or physical abuse is unfair, but it happens.

Homeless people are also very vulnerable to anyone needing a quick buck. This is especially true with homeless runaways, who are constantly being tricked, lied to, and abused by people who want to make money off their bodies. The kids end up prostituting themselves just to make money for food.

The perils of being homeless should be enough to encourage us to work to solve the situation, especially when these people did not choose to be homeless. When we understand and can empathize what it's really like, then we've taken the first step towards ending homelessness.

win, lose & DREW

CHAPTER EIGHT:

LET THEM EAT TARTS:
THE PUBLIC'S ATTITUDE TOWARDS THE HOMELESS

"**T**hey don't want to work."

"They want to be homeless."

"They don't have good work habits."

"They just want a free ride."

"If we make it too easy on them, then it will encourage them to depend on us instead of getting their act together."

"It's their own fault; why encourage it?"

"Homeless people are just that way because they're too lazy to work for a fair wage. Why don't they go get a job?"

These are just a few of the stereotypical comments by people who have not taken the time to understand what homelessness and homeless people are all about. The typical comments show that most Americans believe homeless persons to be "bag ladies" and drunken men sleeping in downtown doorways. They also believe that the fault lies with these people, in some flaw in their character.

Attitudes towards homeless people generally reflect an insensitivity to their pain. They're often seen as lazy, incompetent, and quick to ask for a handout. They are described as under-deserving rather than unfortunate. The public fears that freebies will encourage sloth and maybe even crime.

Being homeless means trying to cope day by day, and having to face an

**At a picnic feeding the homeless, this man protested
that the homeless should be kept out of the park.**
Photo: Sarah Gorder

uncaring public just adds another burden. Gloria Kangas, a woman who has been homeless, left this poem on the bulletin board of the American Red Cross Shelter in Colorado Springs:

> We're living at the Red Cross shelter
> Among a lot of friends.
> Each of us under different circumstances
> On which our incomes depend.
> We don't enjoy living here
> But we're grateful for a home
> Where we can try to find a job
> And do things on our own....
> It's a wonder we maintain our sanity
> Ask anyone here at the shelter
> How we get through the struggle and torment
> Without screaming and losing our tempers.
> If you don't believe what I'm saying
> Come and visit us a while
> Then instead of offering rude remarks
> Try giving us a smile.

Not only does the public hold this attitude, but so do many public officials and social workers. And the hardest part to deal with is the "fault clause"—that is, believing that people are homeless because it's their own fault. When we blame someone for their own situation, then we excuse ourselves from helping. This tendency to stereotype homeless people makes the situation even more difficult to solve.

MEAN-SPIRITED ATTITUDES & HARASSMENT

Just look at this list of typical attitudes by some of our prominent citizens:

✻ *Charleston (WV) Gazette,* April 13, 1986, "Attack deep causes, advocate urges". Kim Hopper, a founder of the National Coalition for the Homeless, cited President Reagan as saying that homeless people prefer living on the streets and Attorney General Edwin Meese as saying that people eat in soup kitchens because it is cheap.

✻ *Des Moines (IA) Register,* October 25, 1986, "Homeless want street life, HUD secretary says". US Housing and Urban Development Secretary Samuel Pierce Jr. said that 70% of the people on the streets want to be there. Commenting on the statement were Dean Wright, vice president of the Des Moines Coalition for the Homeless, who said, "That's the most absurd statement I've ever heard." And Reverend Bob Cook, also of the Coalition, said of Pierce, "Obviously, he's part of the problem."

✻ *Topeka Capital-Journal,* February 16, 1986, "Homeless still a problem in Topeka". The director of the community relations department for the Topeka Police Department claims homeless people have found that Topeka "is not a free ride".

* *Hartford (CT) Courant,* February 8, 1986, "Report opposes opening of city-run shelters for homeless". City Manager Alfred A. Gatta said that opening more shelters would simply attract more homeless people to the streets of Hartford.

* *Las Vegas Review Journal,* March 23, 1986, "Police target homeless". City leaders were pleased to report an increased number of arrests being made for vagrancy, loitering, and similar "crimes". Homeless advocates plea police harassment.

* *Easton (PA) Express,* October 21, 1986, "Lehigh Valley study: Homelessness worst in Easton". Reverend Dave DeRemer compiled a study on homelessness and cast blame on young, "irresponsible" families.

* *Tempe (AZ) Tribune,* March 20, 1988, "Lawmakers: Budget woes leave homeless out in cold." Arizona Senate President Carl Kunasek said, "The homeless issue is not of sufficiently high priority at this point to have somebody working on it."

Various cities have also been found lacking in compassion for homeless people. While visiting Atlanta in late 1986, I noticed a debate taking place about whether or not the city should institute a "safeguard zone" around the center city. The supporters of this idea wanted stricter enforcement of loitering laws (of which Atlanta had none), stricter enforcement of panhandling laws, designing public benches to discourage sleeping on them, and possibly the reinstatement of public drunkenness laws or a mandatory treatment for alcoholism.

They even went as far as to recommend that homeless people *be issued special identification cards and be transported to city prison farms!* This zone would, in effect, cause severe harassment of homeless people.

Reverend Joanna Adams of the Central Presbyterian Church in Atlanta said, "To enforce ordinances against sleeping seems to be a very mean-spirited approach; we're going to arrest people for the crime of being tired."

The obvious constitutional challenges to these laws luckily prohibited their enactment, but the fact remains that many people were in favor of the zone proposals.

In Las Vegas, city officials encouraged arrests of homeless people for misdemeanors such as loitering. Los Angeles' Major Tom Bradley called for a "clean-up" campaign in Skid Row areas, which resulted in raids on the area. Des Moines was also accused of trying to harass homeless people by ordering 30 men to leave a shelter because of overcrowding. A Carpinteria, California agency told homeless people to head to Santa Barbara to sleep, in effect telling them, "You're not wanted here."

People have been repeatedly thrown off private and public land where they were living in tents and make-shift dwellings. In Phoenix, they were ordered to leave the Salt River that runs through the city and adjacent suburbs. Chevron Oil ordered homeless people to vacate a vacant piece of land near Nashville. Outside Pompano Beach, people living in a tent city were ordered to pack up and leave.

Certain social agencies have been equally mean-spirited when dealing with homeless people. The New Jersey law requires that people prove that they are homeless for reasons completely beyond their control. This is called the "fault clause" and means that the social agencies are put in the position of trying to determine if a homeless person is "at fault" before giving any aid.

This clause puts social workers in an adversarial position. Karen Olson of the Interfaith Council for the Homeless of Union County, New Jersey, said, "Welfare workers tell a person receiving a minimum wage or public assistance they could have foreseen their homelessness and done something about it."

The result is that only persons left homeless due to a fire or other similar occurrence are given assistance.

Other social workers feel that making it hard on homeless people, their motivation to be self-sufficient will be increased. Some have told people that they were "criminally negligent" for not being able to provide a home for their children. Instead of compassion, these social workers are trying to use amateur psychological evaluations of homelessness.

GUILTY-GIVING

Some people help poor people, not out of compassion, but out of guilt. They feel lucky for their own comfortable lives, but nervous about the fact that some other people have so little. People who give because they feel guilty are doing it more out of fear than out of love.

As Father Ritter says in *Covenant House,*

> The problem with guilty giving is that it doesn't do anybody any good. To give to the poor without love for the poor poisons both the giver and the gift. Guilty giving doesn't reach out to the poor to share with them our own goodness and riches; it just erects a wall between us and the poor over which we throw our gift to them because we don't want to feel their pain, to sense their closeness to us.

Equally as shallow are those who only help the poor and unfortunate at Christmas. True, it's important to be generous with the needy during the holidays. But why stop after this joyous season is over? Compassion must be a year-round feeling.

"WE WANT A HAND-UP, NOT A HAND-OUT!"

Contrary to popular opinion, homeless people want independence. They want the same things everyone else wants; they have the same ideals and the same goals. They want dignity and a nice place to live and they are willing to work for it.

Only 5% of homeless people chose to live on the streets. The rest are put there through unfortunate circumstances or because of lack of basic facilities—low income housing or community mental health treatment. *It's not their fault,* as so many people would like to imply.

Half of the homeless people are families, another third need mental health treatment, and another large group are runaways.

These people did not chose homelessness!

One of the criticisms of homeless people is that they don't want to work. But studies of poverty have shown that poor people do want to work, that they view work as a positive thing. There are no cultural differences in the way that they see work. Sometimes they have been less successful than a non-poor person, but that doesn't mean that they value work itself any less.

But work orientations have very little to do with homelessness as it exists today. That doesn't explain the homeless runaways and the mentally ill homeless.

> **The bottom line is that old stereotypes do not apply, and in order to get on with solving this problem, we have to throw away those tired old attitudes. Let's not be the type of people who refuse to act because of ignorance or smugness.**

We have to view homelessness as it really is, and then share in the positive steps towards making this country what we always hoped it would be—the land of opportunity where all people are created equal—where every person has a home and food regardless of social class or family relations or mental proficiency.

Long lines for food are becoming altogether too familiar.
Hunger does exist in America.

Photo: Courtesy of the Salvation Army.

CHAPTER NINE:

POOR ∽ HUNGRY ∽ HOMELESS
THE REAL FAST TRACK

There are more than 35 million Americans living in poverty. That's about 15% of the total population. Since 1980, poverty in America has increased 20%. One in seven Americans lives in poverty.

The worse part of these statistics is that the pain is invisible.

These numbers don't show the misery of watching your children go to bed crying because they are hungry. They don't show the hopelessness of being evicted from your apartment because you can't pay the rent, and then end up sleeping on the street or in some city shelter.

It's probably inescapable in any economic system that some people will be poorer than others. But when those poor people are very hungry, and even many are homeless, a compassionate country will do its best to ease the pain.

In the 1960's, Lyndon Johnson executed his "war on poverty". He intended to give a helping hand to people on the lowest economic level. There were widespread reports at the time of epidemic hunger in the United States. The war on poverty was started to end this hunger.

133

In the 1970's, there appeared to be less hunger. Although many people were still poor, they usually had channels for obtaining food.

In the 1980's, we started seeing rampant hunger again, and this time we also started seeing homelessness in epidemic proportions. Now poor people are not only very very hungry, but they are also living on the streets. Tent cities have popped up resembling the Great Depression. Shelters are overflowing. Soup lines are long enough to wind around city blocks.

What happened? Why did efforts started in the 1980's seem to help, then diminish altogether?

We're making the poor, poorer! First poverty, then hunger, then homelessness.

WE'RE MAKING THE POOR-POORER!

HUNGER IN AMERICA 1980'S

The recent hunger epidemic of the 1980's started being observed in 1982 by the US Conference of Mayors survey. Numerous studies started being made. They were:

1. US Conference of Mayors Survey	October 1982
2. United Church of Christ Report	January 1983
3. US Department of Agriculture "Case Studies of Emergency Food Programs"	May 1983
4. Center on Budget & Policy Priorities "Soup Lines & Food Baskets	May 1983
5. US Conference of Mayors "Hunger in American Cities"	June 1983
6. Salvation Army of America Report	June 1983
7. US General Accounting Office "Public & Private Efforts to Feed America's Poor"	June 1983
8. National Council of Churches, Work Group on Domestic Hunger & Poverty	August 1983
9. Bread for the World, Hunger Watch	September 1983
10. US Conference of Mayors "Responses to Urban Hunger"	October 1983
11. Food Research & Action Center "Still Hungry"	November 1983
12. Kennedy report to the Committee on Labor & Human Resources of US "Going Hungry in America". Kennedy said, "There is clear, undeniable, authoritative evidence of widespread and increasing hunger in America."	December 1983
13. Harvard School of Public Health "American Hunger Crisis"	February 1984

14. Citizens Commission on Hunger in New England
    "American Hunger Crisis: Poverty & Health in
    New England"   February 1984

15. Save the Children/American Can Company "Hard
    Choices"   September 1984

16. US Conference of Mayors "The Urban Poor and
    the Economic Recovery"   September 1984

17. Food Research & Action Center "Bitter Harvest" November 1984

18. Physicians Task Force "Hunger in America"   1985

19. US Conference of Mayors "The Status of Hunger
    in America"   April 1985

20. US Conference of Mayors "The Growth of
    Hunger, Homelessness, & Poverty in America's
    Cities"   January 1986

21. US Conference of Mayors "The Continued
    Growth of Hunger, Homelessness, and Poverty
    in America's Cities"   December 1986

The evidence has been overwhelming. The most notable report,"Hunger in America" by the Physicians Task Force, drew three major conclusions:

☆ Hunger is in epidemic proportions all across the nation. They found extensive hunger in every city and every state. Twenty million Americans go hungry at least part of every month. There is ample evidence of people starving to death in this country. Over half of the hungry people are families with children. Other hungry people are the elderly on fixed incomes, American Indians, unemployed factory workers, and surprisingly enough, former farmers.

☆ Hunger in America is getting worse and never in the last 50 years has hunger in this nation spread so rapidly. Food programs have reported increase in demand of 75% to 400% in every major city.

☆ Hunger is a result of federal policies because programs which ended hunger in the 1970's have been weakened.

The conclusions drawn by the Physician Task Force have been supported by the periodical surveys of the US Conference of Mayors. At least twice a year they issue reports on the continued growth of hunger, homelessness, and poverty in America's cities. They have found that the need for emergency food assistance is growing, and that at least 23% of the time the need goes unmet. Cities reported:

☞ Boston: "Because of the great demand for food, programs run out of food and out of funds."

☞ Charleston: "The agencies providing pantry assistance frequently run out."

☞ Kansas City: "Resources are being stretched to their utmost limits, as evidenced by the fact that 1/3 of the local pantries are providing less than a 3-day supply of food."

☞ New Orleans: "Many of the emergency food assistance facilities that were able to meet the demand now have to turn people away because the demand is so much greater."

☞ San Francisco: "The number of feeding sites has not increased, but the number of persons needing such services has."

REAGAN DENIES HUNGER

Interestingly enough, as reports of hunger were increasing in the mid-1980's the administration was denying that hunger could exist in this country. In 1984, the President's Task Force on Food Assistance said that, "General claims of widespread hunger can neither be positively refuted not definitely proved."

Reagan himself, in a memorandum to Attorney Edwin Meese, said that he was "perplexed" by reports of hunger because the poor were eligible for food stamps. And Edwin Meese denied that hunger existed in America as an identifiable problem, and said that his "considerable information" showed that many people in soup lines didn't need to be there.

Later, politically-based attacks were made on the integrity of the fine Harvard doctors who traveled America to report on "Hunger in America". President Reagan claimed publicly that the poor were just too ignorant to know where to get food.

At the same time other pro-administration politicians were saying:

✎ Senator Jesse Helms of North Carolina doubted there was hunger in America. "There is simply no objective, rational, or scientific basis for this perception of hunger in America."

✎ Senator Robert Dole of Kansas said, "There has been no documentation of nationwide 'hunger' problems unless one accepts frequently biased media reports."

✎ Secretary of Agriculture John R. Block said that "poor people shouldn't starve but they shouldn't have a very nice life either; certainly not anything resembling the kind of life the rest of us want."

But the rest of the country was seeing hunger in their cities. Nashville's Mayor Robert H. Fulton pleaded, "Please tell Mr. Meese and the White House that there is hunger in America!"

MORE HUNGER, LESS ASSISTANCE

How could Reagan be so "perplexed" about hunger in America? Between 1982 and 1986, $12.2 BILLION was cut from federal nutrition programs, of which $7 BILLION was cut from the food stamp program. School lunch programs have been cuts $5.2 BILLION.

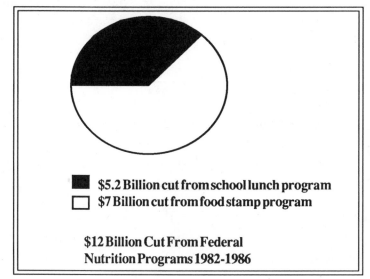

■ $5.2 Billion cut from school lunch program
☐ $7 Billion cut from food stamp program

$12 Billion Cut From Federal
Nutrition Programs 1982-1986

The cuts have resulted in less money for the elderly and disabled's food programs, less in the WIC program (Supplementary Food Program for Women, Infants, & Children).

As the hunger & poverty increase, the number of people receiving food stamps has remained the same.

Teachers of the Head Start Programs worry about the long lists of children on their waiting lists because the children already enrolled are so hungry, and many seem to get nourishment only at school. Of the children already enrolled, 20% come in Monday morning asking for an extra breakfast, indicating they have had little to eat over the weekend.

The amount of money given to a person through the food stamp program

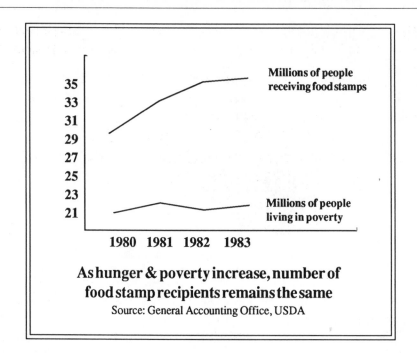

35
33
31
29
27
25
23
21

Millions of people receiving food stamps

Millions of people living in poverty

1980 1981 1982 1983

As hunger & poverty increase, number of food stamp recipients remains the same
Source: General Accounting Office, USDA

was originally based on a "thrifty food plan". That means that it was designed to help people obtain food if they did not waste the money on frivolous types of food. However, the amount a person now receives has been eroded by inflation and increased sales taxes.

The average recipient received $44 a month, or 49 cents a meal. Try providing a nutritious meal three times a day for a month for 49 cents a meal!

Similar to other social programs, the cutbacks in the nutrition programs place the agencies in an adversarial position. It has become much harder to qualify for food aid. Eligibility standards have been altered and benefit levels have changed. All of the mean-spirited tactics mentioned in the next chapter are used, plus a few more.

The Reagan administration was able to make such drastic cutbacks in these food programs by claiming that there was rampant "fraud". Exaggerated examples were given to the media to prove their point. Some critics who are close to the subject believe that these "fraud" examples might even have been plants by Reagan supporters. Not only have they succeeded in reducing the amount of the national nutritional programs, but they have also succeeded in keeping good people from applying for needed aid. These people are often afraid of making a mistake on the complicated forms, and are afraid of being prosecuted. Signs have been posted in some food stamp offices saying:

WARNING: We prosecute food stamp recipients for intentionally making false statements.......

An Alabama Food Stamp Supervisor, Sarah Wunn, told how the federal government made them stop their outreach program. They are no longer allowed to try to locate people who need food. Instead, they have to do more paperwork because the name of the game is saving money.

LAND OF PLENTY
Provides only 49 cents per meal
for its neediest citizens

HUNGER AND HOMELESSNESS

I t's no wonder that homelessness is of epidemic proportions. Poverty is increasing. Hunger is increasing. We're making the poor, poorer! And the ultimate poverty is homelessness.

At a picnic to feed some of Arizona's homeless, Ken and Meg Seaman of Phoenix showed their support. Ken said, "I think it's unfortunate that we can afford to spend billions on weaponry and bombs and things of destruction, and we can't find a few dollars to feed these people who need it so badly."   Photo: Sarah Gorder

Lullabye

by Mary Goings

Mamma, I'm hungry...give me some bread?
Hush, Child, man's gone to the moon.
I'm hungry Mamma. What does it mean to be dead?

The wind's blowing, Mamma, and I'm so cold.
Hush, Child...man's gone to the moon.
Mamma, you're tired and your face looks so old.

Why did Johnny go, Mamma? Why did he go?
Hush, Child. Man's gone to the moon.
Why, Mamma, why? We all loved him so.

"Feed me, Mamma, feed me," that's what he said.
Hush, Child, man's gone to the moon.
You're crying again, Mamma...your face is all red.

I'm so hungry, Mamma. Why is there nothing to eat?
Hush, Child...man's gone to the moon.
Only some milk, Mamma? Some bread? Maybe some meat?

I'm so tired, Mamma, and it's not even night.
Hush, Child. Man's gone to the moon.
Why do I feel sleepy, Mamma? So sleepy and light?

Oh, I want to play, Mamma...to run...and have fun.
Hush, Child...Man's gone to the moon.
Where did the sun go, Mamma? *Where is the sun?*

Rest in Peace, Child.
                    Man's gone to the moon!

Mary Goings is a South Dakota poet and co-author of the book *Womansight*.

ED FRESKA, Los Angeles Times Syndicate

Cartoon courtesy of Ed Freska

CHAPTER TEN:

WHO'S TO BLAME?

Except for the family pressures that cause teenagers to become homeless runaways, the bulk of the problem of today's homelessness is due to governmental failure. The National Coalition for the Homeless, in November, 1987 report, said succinctly,

> **Federal policies over the past few years have caused and exacerbated mass homelessness. Massive cutbacks in federal housing programs have literally squeezed poorer Americans from their homes. At the same, welfare programs also have been cut, forcing poorer Americans to choose between paying the rent and putting food on the table.**

Quite frankly, the poor economic conditions combined with the cutback on low-income housing and mismanaged social service agencies, have literally and figuratively pulled the rug out from under the poor. Persons once considered "poor" are now not only hungry, but homeless.

Even the administration can no longer claim a "safety net" effect from the various social programs, because most are so poorly coordinated and underfunded that they are virtually ineffective.

FACTOR #1: POOR ECONOMIC CONDITIONS

For the past decade and a half, real income for America's poorest families has fallen dramatically due to recession and unemployment. Lower wages and fewer jobs are strong contributing factors to homelessness. Jobs that once were secure have been slashed by factory cutbacks or an industry's recession.

Prime examples were first the auto workers in Detroit, followed by massive layoffs in California's Silicon Valley, and now severe problems in oil-producing areas such as Houston. The farm crisis in the Midwest and a recent troubled potato economy in Maine have added to the economic problems.

People who once held steady jobs in these areas often found their whole lifestyle changed dramatically because they had to try to find jobs in a depressed economy. They had to take whatever job was available, often at half the pay they had been getting. Naturally, it was not enough to make the house payment or the rent that they had been paying previously.

When these people take a cut in pay, people who were already in these low-paying jobs found tough competition. It's a sorry enough situation to have to take society's lowest paying jobs, but when it's difficult to even find one because everyone is needing them, then it's even worse.

So what happens is a shift—middle class blue collar people taking minimum wage jobs, and people already at the poverty level get shoved right out—and the safety net of social services that was supposed to help is full of holes.

We have a whole class of "working poor" that earns so little and receives so few benefits that homelessness is only a crisis away. A little illness, a little mechanical failure, a little family problem—these are all that lie between the working poor and the street.

"The almost-homeless have a really hard time negotiating the system and getting any help at all from it," says Louisa Stark of the National Coalition for the Homeless. If a person is having a hard time making ends meet, there's often nowhere to turn. They can't get help until they're actually out on the street and then there's not enough help available.

The administration has claimed an "economic recovery" over recent years, supposedly from the last recession. (Some might argue that it's been one giant continuous recession since the early 1970's.) In spite of the government's claims, nearly nine out of ten of the cities responding to the US Conference of Mayor's report said that the "recovery" has not helped the hungry, the homeless or other low-income people.

The Mayor's report also said that the number of poor persons in responding cities increased in two out of three cities. Seven cities specifically cited economic factors as a principal cause of homelessness. San Francisco officials said that "fixed and low income have not kept pace with increasing costs of living."

Thus serious income erosion is the first step in making people homeless.

FACTOR #2: LACK OF LOW-INCOME HOUSING

C ombine economic conditions with the lack of affordable housing and—
Abra Kadabra! A homelessness crisis.

What happened?

Public housing projects were first federally funded in the 1930's, the Depression Era. Then Lyndon Johnson instituted a "war on poverty" during his administration, and building subsidized low-income housing was part of the plan. Fewer than half of the six million housing units he believed were needed in 1968 were ever built. In the late 1970's and in the 1980's, construction of low-income housing slowed dramatically. In 1979 there were only 203,000 units constructed or renovated, and in 1983, only 53, 000.

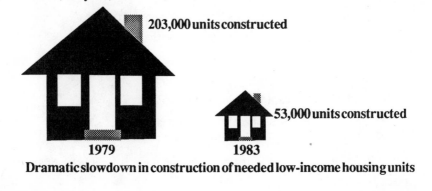

203,000 units constructed

53,000 units constructed

1979   1983
Dramatic slowdown in construction of needed low-income housing units

Yet millions of people need this housing. Two-thirds of people who need subsidized housing do not have it. The demand for low-income housing increased in all but three cities of the US Conference of Mayors report, and 76% of the survey cities identified the lack of affordable housing as the main cause of homelessness. Yonkers officials said that "lack of new housing construction in the rental range affordable to low and moderate income residents and the loss of existing affordable housing either through condemnation or gentrification" were the principal causes of homelessness in Yonkers.

"There are not enough low-income houses. That's the main problem," said Robert Mitchell of The United Way agency.

> "There are not enough low-income houses. That's the main problem."

The average wait for assisted housing is 18 months, according to the US Conference of Mayors. However, no more names are being added to the waiting lists in 68% of the cities because of lack of housing to place people. Keep in mind that averages can be deceiving, as shown by this dramatic list:

- ✍ New York City's waiting period is 18 years.
- ✍ Miami's waiting period is 20 years.
- ✍ Baltimore's waiting period is 8 years, and there are 40,000 families that have been on the list since 1979.
- ✍ Savannah, GA's waiting period is 4 years.
- ✍ Indianapolis' waiting period is 3 years.
- ✍ Seattle's waiting list had 5,500 families in 1985.

The turnover in this type of housing is very slow and there is little hope of actually getting placed.

Linda Fillip, housing coordinator for the Red Cross in Cleveland, Ohio, found that in 1986 she was able to place in affordable housing only 205 of the 1586 homeless people who came to her for help. Directors of the regional Emergency Shelter Coalition asked that the Cuyahoga Metropolitan Housing Authority make available 3,000 of its vacant housing units for these homeless people, but there was no money for renovation. Since that time, the housing crisis has even worsened.

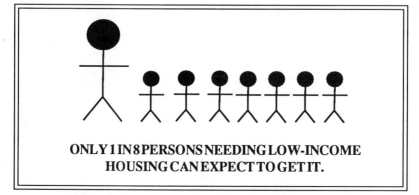

ONLY 1 IN 8 PERSONS NEEDING LOW-INCOME HOUSING CAN EXPECT TO GET IT.

Why is there so little low-income housing available? As a government-subsidized program, it needs government funds in order. But the monies have been cut. "Our sense is that developers would be glad to build affordable housing, but they can't do it without subsidies," said the Seattle Emergency Housing Services' spokesman. Seattle alone lost 70% of its downtown low-income housing since 1960—about 17,000 units.

Federal housing subsidies have been cut from $32 billion in 1980 to a mere $8 billion in 1988, according to Jonathan Kozol, author of *Rachel and Her Children,* a look at New York City's homeless families staying in the Martinique Hotel.

Another problem about low-income housing is that is has proved expensive for the government to build these units, because under the Davis-Bacon Act, government contracts must pay workers the region's "prevailing wage", which is usually top union scale. Often private industry can provide the units at a fifth of what a government project would cost. For instance, the Burnside Consortium renovated 450 units in Portland, Oregon, for costs of $6,000 to $9,000 a unit, less than a fifth of what most government renovations cost.

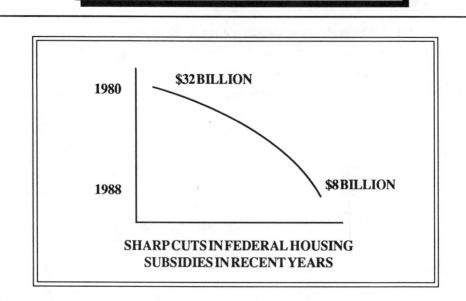

1980 $32 BILLION

1988 $8 BILLION

**SHARP CUTS IN FEDERAL HOUSING
SUBSIDIES IN RECENT YEARS**

While thousands in the city are homeless, Chicago has 6,000 empty public housing units but says it has no money to fix them. One homeless woman asked, "What are they keeping them for—souvenirs?"

At a time when less units are being built or renovated, many are being torn down. In North Carolina, the Charleston Housing Authority decided to close and sell the Ben Tillman Homes in North Charleston. Yet all of the public housing is filled and the Charleton Housing Authority is not accepting any new applications. In Yonkers, New York, the loss of existing affordable housing is a major factor in homelessness. Salt Lake City officials indicated that many low-cost housing units have been demolished.

Gentrification has been blamed for the loss of many low cost housing projects. Gentrification is similar to urban renewal, and is defined in the *Oxford American Dictionary* as "a movement of middle-class families into an urban area causing property values to increase and having the secondary effect of driving out poorer families." In many cities, there has been a reversal of the trend for people to move out to the suburbs. Now "yuppies" and other middle-class families want to move back into the center city. So private contractors profit by renovating building formerly occupied by low-income families, and then leasing them out or selling them to middle-

> "What are they keeping these empty units for—souvenirs?"

class families for more money.

Other times the buildings are renovated for other uses, like perky restaurants and boutiques. Many cities have an "Old Towne" area in the center city, like Albuquerque, Orlando, and Omaha where customers are attracted to businesses relocating into renovated old warehouses and depots. In Baltimore, there are fewer inexpensive boarding houses for low income people because the building have been renovated for other purposes.

The general public has a belief that once low-income is subsidized and built, then it will be there forever. But that's not true. The contractor building the units is obligated to lease the buildings for low-income use only for a limited number of years. Once his obligation is up, the building may be used for other purposes. An interesting phenomenon is that many of these obligations are expiring now, and there will be many many more expiring in the next ten years.

Therefore the picture becomes very very clear. There are fewer units being built, and many are being torn down or renovated for purposes other than moderately price residential housing.

What has happened then, is a net loss in the actual number of units available at affordable prices, while the demand is increasing due to economic factors.

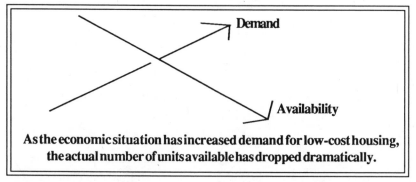

As the economic situation has increased demand for low-cost housing, the actual number of units available has dropped dramatically.

FACTOR #3: LACK OF NEEDED SOCIAL SERVICES

There is a desperate need for social services that is not being met by government agencies, specifically in the areas of:

❑ Community-based mental health services
❑ Day care and job training services for working mothers of low income
❑ Health care for pregnant low income women
❑ Adequate income maintenance programs and food stamps

People who do not need these services almost always assume that it's so available and so easy to get help if you need it. But that's just not true. First of all, the funding has been cut so drastically in many areas of social services that the money is just not enough to cover the need, whether it be health care or food stamps. Secondly, the agencies have generally adopted an adversarial position, meaning they make it as hard as possible to get help, no matter how desperately you need it.

Thirty-two percent of the cities in the Conference of Mayors report mentioned that income maintenance programs are not sufficient. In lay terms, there is not enough welfare money. Specifically:

✳ Seattle officials said that "the welfare benefits in the State of Washington are set at only 65% of the minimum budget needed by a low-income family."

✳ San Francisco officials said that "benefits are not of sufficient levels to last the whole month."

✳ Chicago noted the problem of "inadequate income maintenance" as a major factor in homelessness.

✳ Detroit said that the average rental unit is $322 but the average AFDC (Aid to Families with Dependent Children) payment is about

$194. On average, only 72% of the rent obligation is covered by the social service allotment of $140.

And since the money just is not available, the social services agencies have often been in an adversarial position in treatment of their clients. In other words, they make it as hard as possible to get anything. Examples are:

☞ "Fault clauses" in policies that say, in effect, "if you are at fault for becoming homeless, then we cannot offer you help." In New Jersey, homeless people had to prove that they were homeless for reasons completely beyond their control before they could qualify for aid. Social agencies tell a person that they could have foreseen their homelessness and done something about it. Only a family that is homeless because of a fire or other accidental occurrence could qualify for aid.

☞ The regulations are making it more difficult to qualify for aid programs. For instance, you might be homeless but working. Your income could disqualify you for any aid that would help you get back into housing.

☞ Catch 22 rules like needing an address to get a welfare check, but needing the money before you can rent a place. This means you can't get the money unless you already have a place to get the check. Sometimes applicants are ruled ineligible for aid if they list a local shelter as their address.

☞ Forms are long and difficult to fill out. One state has 21 forms to fill out that total 35 pages in all. All sorts of documentation is required, such as wage stubs, bank statements, social security cards, utility bills, citizenship papers. You are required to come in to fill out the forms and apply in person, even if you have no transportation, are elderly, or are disabled.

☞ There are lots of procedural changes all the time. Every time a new regulation is issued (every ten days on the average) new forms may have to be created. And to top it all, there's the growing phenomenon of "procedural denial" which means that you might be denied aid, not because of eligibility, but because of some detail like you didn't arrive on time or you improperly filled out this form.

☞ The waiting lines are long, and the hassle incredible. It's not unusual to wait 45-60 days to wait for a decision, even if you're on the streets with no money in your pocket. An example of this was shown on "God Bless the Child", an ABC special movie on homelessness, which showed a young homeless woman sitting at a social service agency, having absolutely no assets, but having to wait a lengthy period of time in order to receive any aid.

☞ Agencies that don't tell a client what other channels to follow up to find help. It's common practice **not** to refer people to other places that might be able to help, and **not** to tell you that you might be eligible for something else other than what you ask for.

These social service agencies are a bureaucratic nightmare, to say the least. And worst of all, they're so badly coordinated that even other public employees, such as judges, don't know which agency does what. The agencies are underfinanced, overworked, and incredibly confused.

> The bottom line on dealing with social service agencies
> is that you need to know what you want, what you qualify
> for, who to ask, how to apply, which documents to bring along,
> need it bad enough to qualify but yet not be at fault for needing
> it, and still not need it for at least a month!

WE NEED SOLUTIONS, NOT BAND-AIDS

Congress has acknowledged the massive homelessness in the country, but has offered only band-aid programs to address the problem. In 1986, Congress appropriated $15 million to be spent in 1987 for programs to help the homeless. Then in 1987 the Stewart B. McKinney Homeless Assistance Act was passed and reluctantly signed by the President.

The McKinney Act authorized over $1 billion to be spent in 1987 and 1988 for emergency aid to the homeless.

That sounds good, doesn't it? But, whoa! There's a difference between "authorized" and "appropriated". In government jargon, "authorized" means that the bill has been passed by Congress saying "we should do this". But the money is not really sent anywhere until it's "appropriated".

So let's back up one step. One billion dollars was authorized by the McKinney Act. But only $355 million was actually appropriated (sent to be spent) for 1987. Not only was not enough money appropriated, but this money has not been properly channeled to help the people who need it the most, nor has it been used in ways that could best help these people. The demand for aid still greatly exceeds available funds.

An "Interagency Council" was formed to oversee the implementation of the McKinney Act. That means that there was supposed to be a group of people responsible for seeing that the funds were sent out to the community level by each department receiving it. These federal departments were:

✔ FEMA (Federal Emergency Management Agency)
✔ HUD (Housing & Urban Development)
✔ HHS (Department of Health & Human Services)
✔ GSA (General Services Administration)
✔ DOE (Department of Education)
✔ VA (Veterans Administration)
✔ Department of Agriculture
✔ Department of Labor

The idea behind using these particular agencies was to cover as broad a range of needs as possible. First, FEMA would serve the immediate needs of people—"emergency assistance"—by providing food and shelter on a temporary basis. GSA was to help by finding government buildings that could be used as emergency and transitional shelter. HUD was to provide more permanent housing. HHS was to direct health and mental health services on the community level. DOE would see that the homeless children received an education and the Department of Labor was to see that homeless adults received job training. VA was to help homeless veterans. The Department of Agriculture's job was to provide food and food stamps.

The lack of leadership by the Interagency Council was the first basic problem with the way the McKinney Act was handled. Basically these programs for the homeless did not receive any priority attention from the agencies. They were busy with other things. So busy that the Interagency Council—the bulkhead of the homeless assistance act—met only once: September 29, 1987, five weeks after their legal deadline.

Naturally this resulted in a lack of coordination between agencies on the programs. Simply said, "the right hand didn't know what the left hand was doing". If you talk to a HUD person, they have no idea what HHS is doing. And the GSA person doesn't know what the FEMA person is doing. What happens when there is a lack of coordination is that some very important needs fall through the cracks.

As a coordinated effort then, the McKinney Act was hopeless. But how did each individual department do?

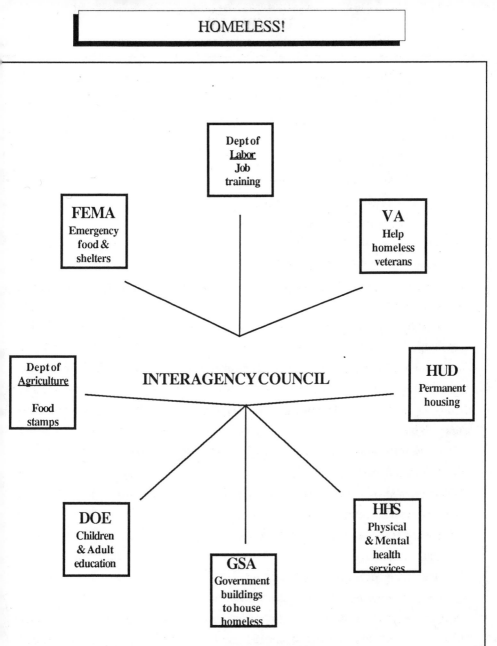

An "Interagency Council" was formed to oversee
the implementation of the McKinney Act.
These departments were responsible for seeing
that the funds reached the community level.

The FEMA programs receive a congratulatory nod for getting the money into the community and actually getting something done. The FEMA branch interacts with local charitable organizations, and they all seem to have been getting something done.

HUD, on the other hand, shows extraordinary slowness in getting the funds to the street. They have delayed distribution for these funds by up to 9 months. HHS takes 5 months to distribute their funds to the community level.

What have these agencies achieved? FEMA has actually provided temporary emergency shelter and food for many homeless people. But not enough. The need is still much greater than the program is providing.

GSA has done little, if anything, to turn over government buildings to shelter the homeless. HHS has provided some health care, but is slow on providing any of the badly-needed mental health care. DOE has been unreasonably slow in doing anything about the education of homeless children and adults. HUD, VA, the Department of Labor, and the Department of Agriculture has done little to help the homeless.

Actually, when you look at the breakdown of funding actually appropriated, it's easy to understand why so little was done. Of the $1 billion authorized by the McKinney bill, only $355 million was appropriated for 1987. And half of this went to the FEMA programs. That's why they were able to provide some emergency help for homeless people—even if it wasn't enough. The other programs that was appropriated significant amounts of funds were the primary health care for the homeless ($30 million) and community service block programs ($35 million). However HUD was appropriated no funds for building transitional or permanent housing, and HHS was given no funds for mental health care.

I hope the picture is getting clearer. What Congress intended to do, I believe, was to start a process to end homelessness. In order to do this long-term, there has to be low-income housing and mental health care at a community level. Congress started out by authorizing programs in this direction.

But the real power, and the real impact, comes when the money is actually appropriated to certain programs. The only programs that actually received money were the emergency programs—the ones that provided temporary food or shelter. These do not end homelessness. They only make it feel less painful for a few days. <u>These are band-aid programs, not solutions.</u>

For real solutions, the money has to be appropriated into channels that actually provide affordable housing, food, and long-term health and mental health care.

The government has all but abandoned helping people. The government looks at poverty in terms of politics, not in terms of people. It's easier for them to acknowledge hunger and homelessness in other nations than right here at home where we're directly responsible.

But Americans do not deserve to be hungry.
They do not deserve to be homeless.
AFTER ALL, WE ARE THE WORLD TOO!

Cartoon courtesy of Mike Peters, *Dayton Daily News*

CHAPTER ELEVEN:

LONG-TERM SOLUTIONS

In his book

Real solutions are long-term solutions to problems, not just band-aid effects. Providing emergency shelters is only the first step, but not the whole path. In fact, continuing to provide only emergency shelters prolongs the problem, and is much more costly in the long-run than real solutions. Keeping people in shelters is often likened to "warehousing", a dead end policy likely to dehumanize people instead of rehabilitating them.

Long-term solutions are permanent affordable housing, job training with placement, health care and community-based mental health care along with group homes for those who need it, ample nutritional programs, homes for runaways that cannot return home, transportation, and supportive social service programs that are flexible, well-coordinated, and properly funded.

Sometimes a transitional program can help ease the person from homelessness to a permanent solution. This "in-between" step should be a really well-coordinated effort to help the homeless person with job training and placement. It should keep in mind that shuffling children from place to place is hard on them, so abrupt changes should be kept to a minimum.

A pictorial illustration of the three states of long-term help is:

HOMELESS!

```
LONG-TERM SOLUTIONS
```

EMERGENCY POLICIES	TRANSITIONAL POLICIES	PERMANENT POLICIES
Shelters	Transitional housing	Permanent housing Group homes for mentally ill and runaways
Food	Food	Nutrition programs
Transportation	Transportation	Transportation
Health Care	Health care Mental health care	Health care Mental health care
	Job training Job interviews Day care Education for children	Employment Day care

REAL SOLUTIONS TO TODAY'S HOMELESSNESS ARE LONG-TERM SOLUTIONS, NOT JUST BAND-AID POLICIES.

EMERGENCY POLICIES

The emergency need is to provide food, shelter, and health care for the people on the streets. The food should be nutritious and tasty, not just somebody else's rejects. The shelters need to be clean, warm, but most of all—safe and humane places. Families should be able to stay together.

Sometimes a temporary solution could be a campground, in a moderate climate. It's often preferable to a shelter, some of which are run-down and flea-infested. But this is viable only if it is regarded as a very temporary plan and if all of the other needed social services are readily available.

A couple of architects have designed individual sleeping units for homeless people. Donald Macdonald of San Francisco built a small weatherproof plywood shelter with windows, a mattress, and a place to hang a hat. He calls it "City Sleeper". These 4' x 4' models cost $500 in materials and are mounted on inverted auto jacks to keep them off the ground. He sees them as a viable alternative to "flea bag hotels" because they provide a humane, private place to sleep that's clean and dry.

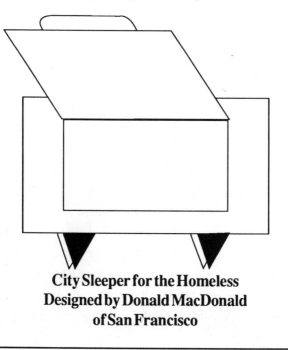

**City Sleeper for the Homeless
Designed by Donald MacDonald
of San Francisco**

Designers S. L. Slaughter and Peter von Gundlach of Tucson created a "Redi-Shelter". This modular 12' x 10' metal, wood, and styrofoam structure costs about $500 and can be built by anyone with pliers and screwdriver. It contains a 1500 watt portable heater which makes the unit 20 to 25 degrees warmer than the outside. One of the advantages of their shelter, they say, is that it can be used to keep people out of the cold and to keep a family together.

Another immediate need is health care. That care must be readily available where it's needed. Some compassionate medical centers, such as the Swope Parkway Comprehensive and Mental Health Care Center in Kansas City, have mobile medical units to care for the homeless. Their "Health Care for the Homeless" team goes wherever it's needed.

Transportation needs to be provided as well as food and shelter, because life does exist outside the confines of one's living space. Without transportation, the world passes us by. In Nashville, the city provided free bus tickets so that homeless people who search for work, child care, and other services can get there.

TRANSITIONAL POLICIES

A transitional program is that which bridges the gap between complete homelessness and permanent housing. There must still be shelter, food, health care, and transportation. But there also needs to be job training and day care. Mental health care or substance abuse programs have to be provided for those who need it.

The Salvation Army has a transitional program called "Motivated Man and Motivated Woman Program". The program's stated goals are "providing individuals with the helping hand they need to return to productive lives by providing shelter, meals, assistance in finding employment, counseling, and much more." Once a job has been obtained, the person is allowed to continue in the program until they have saved up enough money to once again be self-supporting members of the community.

The Salvation Army also has a "Harbor Light Program" to help people recover from alcoholism. This is the largest alcoholism treatment program in the nation. An additional program "The Adult Rehabilitation Program" has long-term treatment for men and women.

Sacramento, California has a Transitional Housing Program that has won an award of merit from the United Nations' International Year of the Homeless Committee (1986). The 6-week program rents a family an apartment for $20 a week, puts them on a strict budget, trains them in money management and nutrition, and requires them to save money for permanent housing.

The rules of this program are strict, but no-nonsense. No pets are allowed, no telephones, no drugs, no overnight guests, and little money for leisure activities. The program has a 65% success rate.

Education for children is an important transitional step. It helps make them feel like they're in the mainstream of life, rather than on the outside looking in. In May, 1988, the Central Arizona Shelter Services started the nation's third accredited school for homeless children. The other two are located in Santa Clara County, California, and in Salt Lake City.

The Phoenix Thunderbirds, a non-profit group that sponsors the Phoenix Open Golf Tournament to help the poor, donated the money to the Phoenix Special Programs for the Arizona school.

PERMANENT POLICIES

The policies that will keep people from becoming homeless persons again are those that help subsidize affordable housing for low-income groups, those that provide sufficient community level mental health care and group homes for the mentally distressed, and social services policies that are adequately funded to provide health, daycare, nutrition, and transportation services.

In order to see that the safety net of social services doesn't fail in the future, we should:

■ Educate the public about homelessness—in churches, schools, community groups. Let them know the "safety net" theory is only as good as the funding available.

■ Encourage more volunteerism for shelters, community social services, benefit events.

■ Coordinate services at a local level. One call should get a person all the information about the services they are needing, instead of a big run-around.

■ Form local coalitions to help homeless people find low-cost housing.

■ Provide lobbyists to influence legislation demanding social services funding at appropriate levels, and once achieved, keep the lobbyists to see that the funding does not drop below that level.

■ Encourage local fund-raising activities for the homeless.

■ Encourage the design, development, and construction of affordable housing.

We must repair the safety net of services in this country, and then follow-up to make sure this tragedy never happens again!

CHAPTER TWELVE:

ONE PERSON CAN MAKE A DIFFERENCE!

Government must ultimately be responsible for ending homelessness, but still there's a lot for individuals to do. This chapter will highlight some of the things that have been done to help the homeless, and show how one person really can make a difference!

Extensive media attention has been given to the plight of the homeless. There have been thousands of newspaper articles written in hundreds of cities over the past couple of years. The nightly news often carries stories of homeless families and individuals. "Nightline" with Ted Koppel has highlighted the issues of homeless families and runaways.

Several made-for-TV movies have been made about homelessness:

☆ "Race Against Winter", a 1986 CBS TV movie was based on the life and career of Mitch Snyder, (played by Martin Sheen) an advocated for the homeless. Snyder drew attention to the plight of Washington DC's homeless by his hunger strikes. Mike Wallace called Snyder "the shepherd of the homeless in Washington."

☆ "God Bless the Child", a 1988 ABC movie showed the situation of a young homeless woman with a child in New York City. The movie ends with the woman abandoning her child so that the child will be placed in foster care—so the child will at least have food and shelter. The movie had classic lines, such as "I may not have an address, but

I still got a stomach" by a woman denied food stamps for lack of a home. Another unforgettable line was the comment by a social worker who told how the US budget was cutting nutrition programs in order to build a sophisticated missile. He said that with that money "I could feed more people than that missile could kill."

☆ "Home Street Homeless", a 1988 CBS after-school special.

CELEBRITIES AND EVENTS

Many celebrities have become involved with the issues of hunger and homelessness. Their social conscience is compelling because of the impact they can have by holding benefits to raise money to help:

☆ Larry Gatlin's single and video "Runaway Go Home" as a part of a nationwide "Project Safe Place." (See Chapter 6.)

☆ Arlo Guthrie often gives concerts to benefit the poor and the homeless, who are frequently the subjects of his songs. Stockton, California, was the sight of one such concert.

☆ Robin Williams, Billy Crystal, Dudley Moore, Steve Allen, Madeline Kahn, Bob Goldthwait, and John Larroquette were comedians for "Comic Relief '87", HBO's November 1987 comedy benefit for the homeless. The 1986 Comic Relief raised $2.6 million that was funnelled to Health Care for the Homeless Projects in 18 cities. A special edition of the Oprah Winfrey show was taped with several of the comedians before the event. HBO picked up expenses for the project. HBO has already announced another Comic Relief for 1988.

☆ Rock star Prince jammed with jazz trumpeter Miles Davis at a Minnesota Coalition for the Homeless fund raiser on New Year's Eve 1987.

☆ Singer Paul Simon lead a group of singers including Grace Jones, James Taylor, and Dion for a New Year's Eve 1987 benefit for New York City's homeless children. Proceeds went to the Medical Mobile Van, which provides health care for the children.

☆ Other celebrities that have spoken out for the homeless are Ed Asner and Valerie Harper. Actress Valerie Harper told a Senate Housing and Urban Affairs subcommittee that aid for the homeless "must be a priority. We must do what is so American in spirit."

Other events that have raised money for the homeless have been organized by individuals who were not celebrities, but people who knew that they could make a difference:

☆ "Hands Around the Capitol", a Phoenix event similar to "Hands Across America" was held May 1987. Participants formed a human chain around the state capitol and sang "God Bless America." The event was organized by the Central Arizona Labor Council, the Arizona Ecumenical Council, and the Catholic Diocese of Phoenix. More than $10,000 was raised which went to the Central Arizona Shelter Services (CASS) in Phoenix and the St. Mary's Food Bank. Mike Bielecki, president of the labor group said, "We raised some money and we raised a consciousness that the problems of the hungry and homeless in the Valley are still with us, and we need to do something in our daily lives to help solve the problems."

☆ "Musicians Benefit for the Homeless" was held in April, 1988 at the Sun Club Lounge in Tempe, Arizona to raise money for the Central Arizona Shelter Services of Phoenix. The door proceeds of $3 per person and 25% of the bar proceeds were donated. Eight bands performed, volunteering their talent. Over $1,000 was raised that night.

☆ "Homeless & Poor People's Peace Walk to Washington DC". A group of half a dozen people are walking from Santa Barbara, California to Washington DC this summer to call attention to the plight of the hungry and the homeless. They started from Santa Barbara in January. I saw them in eastern New Mexico in late April. They hope to have a large group marching with them the final 250 miles and to arrive across from the White House at noon on the day before the Presidential election.

☆ "Bandwagon", a benefit concert by local bands of Providence, Rhode Island, raised more than $5,000 on April 27, 1986. Added to this was the proceeds of an album by the bands. Bandwagon dollars went to various food and shelter projects in the area. Part of the background track of the theme song was:

> Let's give a piece of our hearts
> To keep theirs beating
> Let's starve all selfish thoughts
> And let's start feeding....

☆ "Taste of the Nation" was a Scottsdale, Arizona benefit to aid the hungry and the homeless. Twenty-three of the area's finest chefs as well as numerous restaurants, hotels, and wineries donated their food and services to the May 17, 1988 event. Money was raised through

Homeless & Poor People's
Peace Walk to Washington DC
Eastern New Mexico, April 1988
Photos: Author

food and wine-tasting events. This is one of several events planned by "Share Our Strength", a national network of chefs and restaurants formed in 1984 to raise money for and awareness of the hungry and homeless in the United States and overseas.

HABITAT AND PARTNERS IN ACTION

People who want to make a difference—CAN! Two philanthropists have started housing programs that benefit people less fortunate than them. Millard Fuller of Georgia founded the Habitat for Humanity program and Curtis Cluff of Arizona founded Partners in Action.

Habitat for Humanity was founded in 1976 by millionaire-turned-humanitarian Millard Fuller. The organization's purpose is to provide affordable homes for needy people. In 1986 the group built 500 houses worldwide, with rapid expansion recently because of branches forming all over the country. Even Jimmy and Rosalynn Carter have donated their time to building homes in the Habitat program.

Volunteer labor and donated materials help keep the housing costs down. The program's guidelines requires that the family selected to buy the house must contribute at least 500 hours to building it and must repay the loan through monthly payments. There is no profit made and no interest on the loan. The money repaid is used to build more homes.

Partners in Action was formed by Phoenix landbroker Curtis Cluff after he watched bulldozers demolish a liveable home in order to make room for a new freeway. He was thinking of all of the homeless people down by the Salt River who had only a piece of plywood to call home. He decided that these homes designated for destruction could very well be used to shelter the homeless.

Cluff, with the help of St. Mary's Food Bank director John van Hengle, have been collecting help to salvage those homes. The money comes from private benefactors and the help from volunteers. They can buy these houses at auction for $300 and moving costs are about $15,000. So far the program has salvaged 60 homes and taken parts of another 60. Useable items such as drapes, water heaters, and sinks are stored until needed. Cluff envisions a whole neighborhood of salvaged homes for the homeless.

Top: Jimmy & Rosalyn Carter
working on a Habitat home
Right: Millard Fuller,
founder of Habitat

Photos: © The Christian
Science Monitor/Neal Menschel

ONE PERSON WHO MADE A DIFFERENCE

A person does not need to be rich or famous to make a difference. All you need is caring and then a bit of effort. Several examples have been shown in this book, such as Father Bruce Ritter of Covenant House and Chief Richard Voorhees (both in Chapter Six). As both men could tell you—caring is important, but persistence pays.

A thirteen-year-old boy in Pennsylvania has been helping the homeless for two years. All he had was a social conscience and his two hands. Trevor Ferrell, of Philadelphia, wanders the city streets at night, accompanied by his mother, offering blankets, clothing, food, and comfort to the homeless.

When asked why he helps, Trevor quotes Edward Everett Hale:

> *I am only one, but still I am one.*
> *I cannot do everything, but still I can do something;*
> *and because I cannot do everything,*
> *I will not refuse to do the something I can do.*

He calls his aid "Trevor's Campaign" and it has spread to a small group of volunteers. Local businesses, including 7-Eleven, McDonalds, and Super Fresh Supermarkets have joined Trevor's Campaign with donations of food and money. Thousands of private citizens have also joined in.

Why would an 11-year-old boy from a comfortable suburb become involved with the plight of the homeless? One night he saw a local TV news report, and decided it wasn't fair for people to be living on the streets. He begged his Mom to drive him into the city with his extra blanket and pillow to give to someone who needed it. She was frightened and resisted. But the boy pleaded and finally won out, and the family began nightly treks into the city. Soon he gained regional, then national attention. He has received at least 27 humanitarian awards. Modest Trevor is uncomfortable in the limelight, but still eager to help as many people as possible, so he has accepted invitations to speak in front of various groups.

To help motivate his audience, he tells his favorite story about a rabbi and his students:

The rabbi asked: "How can you tell when night has ended and day has started?" One student said: "When you can see a tree in the distance and tell what kind it is." And the rabbi said: "No." The other student said: "When you can see an animal in the distance and tell if it's a dog or a goat." And the rabbi said: "No. It is when you turn to the person beside you and can tell that he is your brother or sister. Then, you can tell night has ended."

A MARVELOUS ACT OF CIVIL DISOBEDIENCE

Sweet, unassuming Doraine Frick was the last person in the world who would ever consider breaking the law. She wouldn't even want to hurt anyone's feelings, even a little bit. All she wanted to do was to help feed hungry and homeless people.

For two years, Doraine brought homemade soup and sandwiches to Pioneer Park in Mesa, Arizona. She and her partner, Lilia Parlier, prepared food that was paid for through donations of her prayer group. Sometimes they fed as many as 30 people at their weekly Wednesday lunch. They also brought razors, blankets, clothing, toothpaste, and toothbrushes to the park.

Then one day in May, 1988, a note appeared on Doraine's door. The Maricopa County Health Department told her that what she was doing was "illegal under any circumstances" because "all food must come from an approved source and be prepared in an approved kitchen."

Needless to say, when this news hit the media, the public was outraged. Jerry Gillespie, head of the local Tri-City Breakfast Club, a political awareness group, sent a letter to his members asking that they show up the next Wednesday noon with homemade food to feed the needy. He said that this would create a "marvelous act of civil disobedience" to show authorities that the law should not prevent people from being charitable. Radio station KYFI for two days before the event urged people to show up.

At least 150 attended the picnic, most of which were people supporting Doraine's right to feed the poor. About 30 needy people came to the park to eat that day.

So sweet little Doraine Frick's little act of charity became an event of considerable attention. She has become a spokesperson for helping the homeless. She prays that Mesa will provide a shelter for these people because there are no shelters in the city.

Once again, one person can make a difference!

**Top: Doraine Frick &
her partner Lilia Parlier
Left: Feeding the homeless
at Pioneer Park**
Photos: Sarah Gorder

I'M NOT RICH OR FAMOUS BUT I CAN HELP TOO!

The important thing is that you reach out and help in some way. To say that you care isn't enough. Action is much more important than words when it comes to helping others. As Father Bruce Ritter says in *Covenant House:*

> God can appear to a hungry man only in the form of bread. We can be God to the poor by doing what Jesus did—by feeding them, by going among them, by holding out, in our hands, comfort for them.
>
> This is the only way a Christian can find Him, can make his hands Christ's hands. All else is vanity and compromise and untruth. Our hands must feed the hungry, touch and comfort the sorrowing.
>
> All salvation involves a reaching out, a touching. Salvation, like our redemption, is indisputably physical.

Everyone has something they can give; some special way they can help. Examples of how ordinary people can help are:

- ✔ **Architect:** Make designs for Habitat.
- ✔ **Nurse:** Donate health care to a mobile unit helping the homeless.
- ✔ **Teacher:** Volunteer to help teach homeless children.
- ✔ **Mental Health Care Professional:** Donate mental health care for homeless; form therapy groups for the homeless and needy.
- ✔ **Contractor:** Donate materials to shelters, Habitat.
- ✔ **Used Furniture Store Owner:** Donate furniture to transitional living groups.
- ✔ **Store Owner:** Hire a homeless person; donate materials for shelters and Habitat, post bills about activities to help the homeless.
- ✔ **Auctioneer:** Sponsor a benefit auction.
- ✔ **Musician:** Sponsor a benefit concert.

✔ **Bar Owner:** Host a benefit concert.

✔ **Poet:** Write compassionate poetry about hunger & homelessness;
   Read it at poetry society meeting; organize "Poets Helping Homeless".

✔ **Administrative Person:** Form a coalition to find low cost housing
   for homeless; join a coalition to help coordinate homeless agencies.

✔ **Hotel owner:** Set aside a couple of rooms for the homeless at no cost
   or very low cost.

✔ **Average Citizen:** Drive a homeless person to a job interview.
   Volunteer time; Donate money.

   Spread an attitude of compassion about homelessness.

   Join a coalition to help coordinate activities of homeless agencies.

   Form a coalition to find low rent apartments for homeless.

   Volunteer labor for building houses for Habitat.

   Reach out to a family having financial difficulties and help them so
   they don't end up homeless.

   Offer to babysit so a homeless person an get to a job interview or
   to work.

   Convince those around you—your co-workers, employers,
   employees, friends, relatives, neighbors—to do what they can to help.

APPENDIX

US Conference of Mayors
1620 Eye St NW
Washington DC 20006
(202) 293-7330

National Coalition for the Homeless
1439 Rhode Island Ave NW
Washington DC 20005
(202) 659-3319
&
105 E 22nd St
NY 10010
(212) 460-8110

Habitat International
Habitat for Humanity
Habitat & Church St
Americus GA 31709-3423
(912) 924-6935

Community for Creative Non-violence
425 2nd Street NW
Washington DC 20001
(202) 393-1909

This organization has a
National Volunteer Clearinghouse
for the Homeless
Call 1-800-HELP-664
for a computer printout
showing organizations
in your area needing volunteers.

Covenant House
460 West 41st St
New York NY 10036
(212) 613-0300
Nine line for runaways 1-800-999-9999

National Center for Missing/Exploited Children
(212) 634-9821
1-800-843-5678

National Union for the Homeless
2001 Spring Garden St
Philadelphia PA 19130

Partners in Action, Inc.
2980 E Northern, Bldg A
Phoenix AZ 85028

BIBLIOGRAPHY

Brenton, Myron.*The Runaways: Children, Husbands, Wives and Parents*. Boston: Little, Brown and Company, 1978.

Brown, Dr. J. Larry and H. F. Pizer. *Living Hungry in America: The Harvard Physician Task Force on Hunger in America reports on the face of hunger in a bountiful land*. New York: Macmillan Publishing Company, 1987.

Goodwin, Leonard. *Do The Poor Want to Work? A Social-Psychological Study of Work Orientations*. Washington, DC: The Brookings Institute, 1972.

Hampden-Turner, Charles. *From Poverty to Dignity: A Strategy for Poor Americans*. Garden City, NY: Anchor Press/Doubleday, 1974.

Harrington, Michael. *The Other America: Poverty in the United States*. New York: Macmillan Publishing Company, 1962.

Kozol, Jonathan. *Rachel and Her Children: Homeless Families in America*. New York: Crown Publications, 1988.

Leinwand, Gerald. *Hunger and Malnutrition in America*. New York: Franklin Watts, 1985.

Physician Task Force on Hunger in America. *Hunger in America*. Middletown, CT: Wesleyan University Press, 1985.

Ritter, Father Bruce. *Covenant House: Lifeline to the Street*. New York: Doubleday, 1987.

Rousseau, Ann Marie. *Shopping Bag Ladies: Homeless Women Speak About Their Lives*. New York: Pilgrim Press, 1982.

Shorris, Earl, editor. *While Someone Else is Eating: Poets & Novelists on Reaganism*. Garden City, NY: Anchor Press/ Doubleday, 1984.

INDEX

OTHER BOOKS BY BLUE BIRD PUBLISHING

REAL DAKOTA!

REAL DAKOTA! is a book that celebrates the Dakota Centennial in a very special way—it focuses on the people who have made the states strong. It is a unique book about Dakotans—by Dakotans themselves.

The book shows more than the fact that Dakotans are a talented group of people. It shows that they are people with feelings similar to those of any group of people in the world—that is, universal emotions. They are compassionate, hard-working, patriotic, sensitive, and fun-loving. They have their weaknesses, but they are always working towards making things better.

And most of all, Dakotans are striving towards better communications between people, bridging the gaps between cultures and ethnic groups.

ISBN 0-933025-07-6 $11.95

WHO'S WHO IN ANTIQUES

edited by Cheryl Gorder

The only national comprehensive directory of the antique profession! It includes auction companies, show promoters, independent antique dealers, antique mall dealers, periodicals, appraisers, services, authors, publishers, and organizations. Well-organized reference.

ISBN 0-933025-10-6 $14.95

Order form on page 192

MORE BOOKS BY
BLUE BIRD PUBLISHING

HOME SCHOOLS: AN ALTERNATIVE
by Cheryl Gorder

Explores the controversies of home schooling and offers guidelines for parents interested in the alternative. Lists resources and home school organizations. Numerous reviews have applauded the book, including the nationally recognized *Booklist* and *Small Press Review.* The author has been on a national tour of radio and television interviews. She is also in demand by home school groups as a lecturer. Two months on the Small Press Bestseller list. Updated 1987.

ISBN 0-933025-10-6 $11.95

HOME EDUCATION RESOURCE GUIDE
by Don Hubbs

A comprehensive listing of hundreds of important addresses for home schooling materials and resources. Includes: correspondence schools, curriculums, testing services, educational toys and games, newsletters, school supplies, support groups, devotional materials, foreign language materials, library services, handicapped resources, speakers and seminars, and recommended lists. Says Mary Pride in *NEW Big Book of Home Learning,* "The book is a browser's delight...Those dedicated to home schooling, especially home school leaders, will get some mileage out of the *Resource Guide.*"Updated 1988.

ISBN 0-9615567-1-8 $11.95

ORDER FORM

To order more books from Blue Bird Publishing, use this handy order form.

_____ *Homeless! Without Addresses in America* $11.95
_____ *Real Dakota!* $11.95
_____ *Who's Who in Antiques* $14.95
_____ *Home Schools: An Alternative* (revised) $11.95
_____ *Home Education Resource Guide* (revised) $11.95

Shipping Charges: $1.50 for first book.
Add 50 cents for each additional book.
Total charges for books: _____
Total shipping charges: _____
TOTAL ENCLOSED: _____

Checks, money orders, and credit cards accepted.
NAME: _____
ADDRESS: _____
CITY, STATE, ZIP: _____

Please charge my _____ VISA _____ MasterCard
Card# _____
Expiration Date: _____
Signature: _____
Phone#: _____

VISA   **MasterCard**

Send order to:

BLUE BIRD PUBLISHING
1713 East Broadway #306
Tempe AZ 85282

188
18 41